James McBey (1883–1 ... north-east of Scotland ... At fifteen he became .... of Scotland Bank in Aberdeen. An article in *Boy's Own Paper* stimulated his interest in etching, leading him to borrow books from the Public Library and to study at night. McBey carried blocks in his pocket to sketch straight to the metal, and made his first prints at the age of seventeen by using an old mangle as a press.

He left the bank in 1910, and took a trip to Holland to spend the summer with his art. His first exhibition was held in 1911 at the Goupil Gallery in London, where his work sold out and attracted very favourable notices. McBey was taken up by agents and set out to travel, producing work from visits to Holland, Spain, Morocco, Cornwall and the Thames estuary.

Called up in the Great War, McBey continued to draw in his spare time, and became an official war artist for the campaign in Egypt where he remained until 1919, creating hundred of sketches, plates and watercolours. When the 1920s arrived there was a tremendous vogue for etching, and McBey's reputation was at its height. He continued to travel and work, with visits to Holland and Venice, and his work sold for record prices. He married an American, Marguerite Huntsberry, in 1931, and himself became an American citizen in 1942. Later he returned to his beloved North Africa, spending his retirement in Tangier, where his widow still lives.

A *catalogue raisonné* was published in 1925, and Malcolm Salaman produced an illustrated account of his life and work in 1929. McBey's art is represented in the British Museum, the Imperial War Museum, the Victoria and Albert, the Luxembourg Gallery in Paris, and there are major collections of his work in the Boston Public Library, the National Gallery, Washington, and most notably in the James McBey Room and Library at Aberdeen Art Gallery.

The Early
Life of James McBey

AN AUTOBIOGRAPHY

Edited and Introduced
by Nicolas Barker

CANONGATE
CLASSICS

52

First published in Great Britain in 1977 by
Oxford University Press. First published as a
Canongate Classic in 1993 by Canongate
Press Ltd, 14 Frederick Street, Edinburgh
EH2 2HB. Copyright © Marguerite McBey.
Introduction © Nicolas Barker. All rights re-
served.

Illustrations Nos 1, 2, 3, 4, 5, and 11 are reproduced by kind permission of the City of
Aberdeen Art Gallery and Museums Collections. Illustrations Nos 6, 7, 8, 9, 10, 12, 13,
14, 15, 16 and 17 are reproduced by kind permission of Winston Moll.

British Library Cataloguing-in-Publication Data
A catalogue record for this book is available
from The British Library.

ISBN 0 86241 445 8

CANONGATE CLASSICS
Series Editor: Roderick Watson
Editorial Board: Tom Crawford, J. B. Pick

The publishers gratefully acknowledge general
subsidy from the Scottish Arts Council towards
the Canongate Classics series and a specific
grant towards the publication of this title.

Set in 10pt Plantin by The Electronic Book
Factory Ltd, Fife
Printed and bound in Finland by Werner
Söderström Osakeyhtiö

Contents

List of Illustrations

Introduction

James McBey's life was filled with dramatic events and coincidences. They came unsought but not unacknowledged: he recognised them as turning points, links in a chain which, as he looked back, stretched behind him to the Buchan of his birth and youth. His life thereafter was filled with adventures and incidents, the telling of which kept his friends spellbound as he recounted them in his gentle but resonant voice and with the Scottish accent of his birthplace.

Although his life began in bleak, harsh circumstances, the chain of events that took him through so many strange places and unusual meetings did not always lead upward. The story of his early life ends on the brink of his first, spectacular success. The immediate warm reception of his first London exhibition in November 1911 and the quick sale of his prints that followed led to a triumph unbroken, even enhanced, by the First World War, and his new experiences as a war artist. Soon after the war the demand for his etchings was so great that the entire edition would be sold out immediately, to be resold at once at prices that no other living artist commanded. But the market for contemporary etchings ended with the Great Depression and, curiously, saw no revival for fifty years. McBey, unperturbed by the loss of the principal source of his reputation and income, worked for the rest of his life mainly in oils and watercolours. Since his death in 1959, his work has been rediscovered, and there have been an increasing number of exhibitions of it; besides this book, originally published in 1977, his long attachment to Morocco has been celebrated in *James McBey's Morocco* by Jennifer Melville, with Michael Davidson's photographs, published in 1991.

The story of how he came to write down his memoirs of his early life and how, much later, they came to be published is itself dramatic and surprising. After his sudden success in London, interviews and pieces relating to his life as well as his work constantly appeared in the press, and since the early thirties he had been pursued relentlessly by a publisher to write his autobiography. But it was not until after the Second World War, spent in exile from his beloved Morocco in America, that he found the time to embark on it. He had returned to Morocco, but, overwhelmed by the visual richness and the starvation that preceded it, could not find his artistic touch. He turned to writing his life story instead. He began it in the winter of 1947 during a patch of bad weather that made painting impossible. When he had finished the account of his life up to the point where he abandoned his safe but constricted career in the Aberdeen bank and risked his chance as a professional artist, he paused. His wife Marguerite carefully typed out the manuscript for him, and he sent it to his friend and patron, H. H. Kynett, in Philadelphia.

Encouragement was badly needed, but Kynett found the text too bleak and stark. He did not appreciate the spare vigour of the writing, nor the drama of the tale of an artistic talent forcing itself irresistibly through opposed and unyielding surroundings, like water through granite. Without the stimulus of Kynett's sympathy and professional advice, McBey wrote no more. After his death, Mrs McBey, who had from the outset realised the value of what he had written, tried to get it published: Rupert Croft-Cooke was asked to complete it, by writing a continuation; the Aberdeen University Press provided estimates for a privately printed edition of McBey's text alone. But neither availed; the manuscript came to rest in the drawer of a table in the room off his studio in London where he kept the collection of white paper, begun with a view to using it for his etchings, but continued for the pleasure he got from the visual and tactile qualities of paper as such.

In the event it was the paper that broke the deadlock. Mrs McBey offered the paper as a gift to Harvard University, and Roger Stoddard of the Houghton Library there asked me to examine and report on it. I did so, and the outcome was the publication of *The McBey Collection of Watermarked Paper*, a set of portfolios of specimens of the different stocks he had collected, with a *catalogue raisonné* by Colin Cohen. But in the process I happened on the manuscript of the McBey memoir, began to read it idly, and then with ever increasing intensity. It was a winter afternoon that wore on into the evening, but I read until McBey's rough but calligraphic script was all but invisible, not daring to stop and switch on the light lest it break the spell.

As soon as I could I asked Mrs McBey about the manuscript. She told me how it came to be written, and what happened afterwards. It seemed to me unthinkable that such a masterpiece should remain unpublished, and I enquired diffidently if I might try where others had failed. Mrs McBey lent me the typescript, and I laid it before my colleagues at the Oxford University Press. They were as taken with it as I had been. Together, we worked out a scheme with Mrs McBey, that the original text should be printed exactly as it stood, with only a brief epilogue, an outline of his subsequent career, a fragment of what might have been a full autobiography.

This fragment, however, is complete as it stands. As an account of the rigour of life in Aberdeen and Buchan at the turn of the nineteenth century, it is both full and vivid. It also explains exactly how a native talent of exceptional strength was discovered and self-taught, and finally broke out of the shackles of ignorance and an inhospitable background. It is a wholly absorbing story, a small masterpiece, told with economy of words, simple but chosen with immense care.

Originality and economy were gifts that McBey applied not only to drawing, painting, and engraving, but to everything he had to do in life. It is not surprising, then, that he should have mastered the art of writing when he gave his mind to it. The sheets are firmly written in pencil, with few crossings-out or afterthoughts. All the vividness of his speech is preserved, as was the case in his letters, and this gives his writings a freshness which more practised writers will envy. There is every evidence that he would have continued to write the rest of this story with equal zest and assurance. Although the end comes just as he is poised to move to London and begin his professional career, the first part of the story ends in fact as he walks out of the bank for the last time. The journey to Holland immediately after, which he intended only as a break, was so entirely different, opened such wide horizons, both visual and spiritual, that it was the beginning of a new life.

The farewell to Scotland from the battlements of Stirling Castle was like so many other dramatic moments of his life—highly significant and frequently attached to places. They were all religiously entered into his pocket diary in a minute and neat hand. These diaries and his own excellent memory were the material on which he drew in writing the account of his early life.

McBey continued to keep his diaries until his death, and they provided the record of events on which the epilogue was based. Mrs McBey's vivid memory of events recounted by him and, later, shared with her, made it possible to describe the period in more than bare detail, thanks to the careful record made by her and the late Lady Caroline Duff. Even so it is designed only as an attempt to answer some of the questions that McBey's own story raises. A full account of his life and work must wait for another occasion.

The illustrations are an important addition to the narrative. McBey always felt a strong sense of destiny with a compulsion to preserve even the smallest mementoes of his life, including a surprising number of photographs of his family and early life, from the smithy to the bank. These are amplified by some of his own paintings and prints, chosen to represent his work at the time and to provide a visual background to the story. These documents have been largely deposited at the Aberdeen Art Gallery and Museum by Mrs McBey. I am grateful to the Director, Mr Ian McKenzie Smith, and his staff for their continued kindness in making them available. But my principle debt is to Mrs Marguerite McBey, without whose encouragement and determination this work would never have received a first, still less a second, edition. By taking great pains to ensure the accuracy of the text and equal care to prepare and list the illustrations in the first edition, she made a far larger contribution to this book than would appear at first sight. I must also record my gratitude to my former colleagues at Oxford University Press, Catherine Carver and Susan le Roux, for their work on the text.

When *The Early Life of James McBey* first appeared, it was not widely reviewed. But two notices, those in *The Times Literary Supplement* and *The Listener*, both percipiently noticed its classic quality, that it could be fairly compared with any of the great autobiographies of the past. I am delighted that this quality has been recognised by Canongate Press, whose enterprise now offers the reader a second chance to discover the masterpiece.

Nicolas Barker

Buchan, the corner of Scotland projecting into the North Sea beyond Aberdeen, is a stern flat land fringed by rocks and sand dunes, sparsely punctuated by small villages and farms and inhabited by survivors, who extract a grim livelihood from the tough soil.

The scanty trees cluster together for mutual protection, each of them having a character all its own, warped and twisted by vigorous winds and long winters.

The river Ythan gently drains the flat countryside to the east. Its estuary is wide and tidal for four miles, but its exit to the sea is a narrow gap between massive sand dunes. Inland about a mile is Newburgh, a village of austere rough-stone blue-slated houses, a few shops and eight hundred inhabitants who exist precariously on the local produce, mostly oats and barley, almost half the population making a livelihood off the other half.

A mile to the south, on the road to Aberdeen, is a small cottage attached to a blacksmith's shop, occupied in 1883 by William Gillespie. He was an erect, powerful man with a black square beard and had been blacksmith there since 1843. His married son George and a hired man assisted him in the smithy, and living with him were his surviving unmarried daughters Jane and Ann.

On 23 December 1883, at 22 years of age, Ann became my mother.

My earliest recollection goes back to when I was three years old, and is that of an irate grandfather upbraiding my mother in the little garden in front of the house. Dimly I sensed that the discord was connected with me and that he was angry on my behalf. My mother, in a huff, seized my arm and dragged me to the barn, where, seated on a pile of straw, she and I finished eating a bowl of brose she had in her hand.

At the rear of the smithy the ground sloped downwards to the Foveran burn across which my grandfather had constructed a dam with a sluice leading to a turbine. The power generated by the turbine was transmitted up the field to the smithy by a method which my grandfather had himself invented. Geared to the turbine was an iron crankshaft having three arms, to each of which was attached a wire. The three wires moved backwards and forwards over sheaves fixed on eight poles across the hundred and fifty yards to the smithy where there was a corresponding crankshaft geared to the turning lathe. Thus, each wire became a flexible piston rod and connecting rod at each end.

One memorable day my grandfather took me with him to the dam and lifted me down on the sloping cement runway, which was dry except for pools of water left in the depressions. In these were tiny flounders. It amused him to see my delight when, touching them with his staff, they darted about frantically in the shallow water.

The smiths who helped him smoked Bogie Roll tobacco in clay pipes. When new, these were white and elegant but the stems very soon broke or were chewed away, so that the normal appearance of the pipe was of a dirty brown bowl slightly projecting from a thick moustache. The smiths made me believe that pipes grew short naturally as they were smoked. They presented me with a clean, white new one with a fine long stem, filling the bowl with iron scales from the anvils. My childish disappointment at the failure of my pipe to colour or grow short was their daily humour.

Across the road from the smithy was a copse surrounded by a low wall of loose stones. Once when I was trying to climb this wall for faggots a loose stone rolled on to the little finger of my right hand, crushing it. I had not seen blood before and my finger's behaviour astonished me. I hurried to my grandfather who called out for a pan of water. He took his blacksmith's tongs and pulled the flattened edges of my finger back into shape. I watched the process with objective interest. Only when he immersed my injured hand in the ice cold water did I cry out in pain.

On 6 April 1888, when I was four years old, my grandfather died, and his married son George, who helped at the forge, succeeded him. My grandmother, my mother, my aunt and I now moved to a tenement in the village, which, though only a mile from the smithy, I had never seen.

The springy turf of the square mile of links, redolent of aromatic thyme, was so strange and wonderful to me, as hitherto I had seen only tilled fields. Through the gap in the sand dunes lay the sea, flat, crouching, and angry, thrashing itself on the sand to the edge of the world. Its steady muttering drone was the background of sound against the silence in which we all lived.

Curiously enough, my mother was at pains to keep me clean and tidy and would never allow me to go barefooted in the summer like the other boys of the village, which made me feel isolated.

When I was about six years old my mother's eyes began to trouble her and every few months she had to journey to Aberdeen by the horse bus for treatment at the Royal Infirmary.

The relationship between my mother and myself was unusual. She had never shown affection towards me or kissed me and I had been brought up to address her and refer to her as 'Annie', never as 'Mother'. Her attitude seemed to become more and more harsh; she may have been worried about her eyesight.

The eye doctors at the infirmary had prescribed leeches. We got four of those loathsome animals and kept them in water in a glass jar. A strange animosity existed between Annie and my grandmother who, short, stout, and kind, seemed in some way to be afraid of her. Annie would not allow my grandmother to handle the leeches; I never knew why. This became my unpleasant job. Annie laid her head on a cushion on a table. I got one of the leeches in a wine-glass, inverted this on her temple and held the glass until the leech took hold, biting through the skin. Fighting my nausea, I watched it become bloated with the blood it was sucking from my mother. When, gorged, it released itself, I had to transfer it to a saucer in which was a layer of salt which made it spew out its fill of blood. The operation had to be repeated every fortnight or so; soon Annie's temples were pitted with the scars of the leech-holes.

Our library consisted of a Cruden's Concordance, the poems of Thomas Hood and Martin Tupper, a life of Martin Luther, an old Atlas in two volumes with engraved maps of which that of Africa was a fringe of outlandish names enclosing a void of yellow paper, and a large family Bible belonging to my grandmother in which she had written the names of her children with the dates of their births.

The Bible was full of fascinating engravings and from them I formed my childish mind's eye conception of God—a somewhat severe-looking Old Gentleman with flowing white moustache and a long square beard, clad in a blanket respectably draped around His Figure.

The *Life of Martin Luther* had for a frontispiece an engraving of the reformer declaiming in a heroic attitude with his right arm extended high and his left hand spread flat on his chest. My grandmother seeing me studying the engraving said, 'What does it say below? The print is too small for me to see properly.' I read out, 'Martin Luther at the Diet of Worms.' She regarded the engraving with deep renewed interest, then said, 'Puir man. Nae wunner he's hauden his wymie.' (No wonder he is holding his stomach.) We were both puzzled as to why he had undertaken this strange gastronomical effort.

My grandmother had me read aloud to her a chapter of the Bible every night before bedtime. My favourite chapters were the shortest ones. She very soon got wise to this and demanded an additional chapter. Then I fell back on the genealogical chapters of the first book of the Chronicles and haltingly read to her from the listed posterity of Abraham, Jesse, Caleb, etc., the chief men of God, the stock of Saul and Jonathan and the catalogue of David's mighty men. She listened for only a few minutes to the rocky cacophony, then her patience invariably broke and she freed me with the remark, 'You do seem to get the folk with the queerest names to read about. Maybe we have had enough of them for tonight. You'd better go to bed.'

Religiously every Sunday forenoon all the villagers who could walk the intervening mile attended church service—a grim and solemn ritual. A strong smell of confined varnish pervaded the church and lent the service a characteristic flavour.

Each farmer for miles around was known by the name or a contraction of the name of his farm—Pitscaff, Linnie, Saak, Pitgersie, Ardo, Graibadona, Drums, Dubbystyle—and each had his pew. The pews of the prosperous wore cushions; those of the more humble worshippers had no padding on their narrow wooden seats and upright backs.

The entrance was at the extreme front left of those already seated, who thus had an excellent view of the late comers. These self-consciously picked their steps to their pews well aware that the minutest details of their attire and deportment were being carefully noted.

The precentor took his post at the harmonium. The Minister in black Geneva gown and white bands slowly ascended the pulpit, bent his head for a few seconds, and proclaimed the opening psalm. A long placatory prayer followed, then a hymn, then the text (usually from the more ambiguous sentences of St Paul) on which the sermon would be based. The sermon lasted for three-quarters of an hour; the faint rustle of the congregation at the words 'In conclusion . . .' betrayed its relief. Then another hymn, a short prayer, still another hymn followed by a long pause whilst the collection was taken. This was done by the elders of the Kirk, each of whom went to his appointed section bearing a pole like a broom handle with a square open wooden box at the end, like a cigar box minus its lid. Deftly he pushed this along in front of each pew, the meanwhile everyone listened to the fall of the coin into the box. All could tell if the coin was a halfpenny, a penny, or a threepenny piece.

Our minister—the Reverend J. S. Loutit—was determined to change the mode of collection, and at his own expense supplied purple velvet bags with handles which could be passed from hand to hand, quietly in a civilised manner. This created a schism and feeling ran high for months. Nearly half the congregation suspected this to be a ruse of the Devil who had caught the minister off guard.

In the summer the minister's place was taken by visiting clergymen. One of these—a mighty angler—came for the trout fishing year after year and officiated in the pulpit. He was a big man, bald and clean shaven. A long, lipless mouth bisected his massive square jaw. He had an impressive manner of thrusting his upper bulk far forward over his hands clenching the rail of the pulpit and thundering with vehemence the details of Hell. Of him it was told that at the close of one of his lurid descriptions of Hell he intimated to his congregation, 'and when ye are suffering all this, ye will raise your eyes to the Lord and ye will say unto Him, "Oh, Lord, we did not think it would be as bad as this". And the Lord will look down upon ye and in His infinite compassion and mercy will say unto ye, "Well, ye ken noo".'

The service concluded, the congregation formed itself in the churchyard into small knots dictated by friendships or social status and slowly wound its way in an elongated column through the mile of dust, or mud, back to the village. We schoolboys formed groups by ourselves. On one particular Sabbath two others and I were nearing the village, deep in small-boyish criticism of the adults. One of my companions, a year older than myself, said to me, 'I suppose your mother was married but just kept her maiden name?' Being less than eight years old, I had never given the matter a thought, so had no reply to his implied question, but it mystified and perturbed me as to why my mother should be Annie Gillespie and I, James McBey. A total lack of affection or sympathetic understanding between us kept me from asking Annie to explain and I somehow hesitated to ask my grandmother about a matter so personal.

One Sunday afternoon soon after this Annie took me for a solemn walk across the Foveran Links. In the distance, a solitary man was seated on an isolated boulder. He stood up as we drew close and Annie engaged him in conversation. He was tall, thick-set, with dark moustache and close-cropped side-whiskers. Frequently during the ten minutes he and Annie talked, he regarded me with his grey eyes in a curiously penetrating manner but he addressed no word to me. A few minutes after we left him Annie said to me 'That was your father'—a statement meaning nothing to me then.

Sundays were dreary days—days of restraint, inertia and suppression. Every physical action was either permissible or sinful and the Sabbath had a code all to itself. No games were allowed; whistling, because of its association with joy or light-heartedness, was forbidden; even the humming of a secular melody was stopped by 'Is that a tune for the Sabbath?' My grandmother was most perplexed when she learned that the Salvation Army was, in its effort to save souls, successfully setting sacred words to popular profane tunes.

I have heard her relate of the night of the storm which blew down the Tay Bridge on 28 December 1879, a disaster in which eighty persons perished. She had gone out in the gale to look for possible damage and saw the corn stacks blown into the darkness one after the other. On my asking her why the bridge, regarded as an engineering feat, had collapsed, her grave and serious explanation was that the train crossing it at the time was full of sinners, because they were journeying on a Sunday.

Her religious belief was profound, simple, and primitive. To her, God was a Being, just, severe, jealous, irascible, on occasions vindictive, but subject to placation. Her Heaven was an eternity of relief from effort, pain, and worry, entrance to which was to be obtained by the individual conducting him- or herself in this life so stringently as to outwit the Devil. Her Devil was all-pervasive, infernally cunning and most stealthy, and the candidate for Heaven had to be incessantly on the alert against his artful machinations. The enjoyment of anything was subject to intense heart-searching; the moment a task became a pleasure it was a sure indication that the Devil had won another victim.

She so imbued me with terror of the hereafter that, believing I had no chance against such a potent Devil, I secretly prayed to God—her God—that I might live for millions and millions of years. My terror was accentuated in 1892 by my being summoned from a game of marbles in the street, to be present at the death bed of my aunt Jane who had been ailing for many months, of shingles. I have no recollection of her passing, but next day, when told to put my hand on her forehead, I drew it sharply back from the uncanny contact; her brow felt like painted ice.

Our meals were frugal. The function of food was to keep the body alive and working; it was not to be enjoyed, and the changes were rung with oatcakes, white bread, boiled beef, cabbages, kail, carrots, turnips, potatoes, and tea.

As the entrance to the Ythan was difficult for small boats at all times and the gales were frequent in the winter, fish was not plentiful. The grocer kept a stock of dried codfish imported from Newfoundland and on this we fed several times a year. By way of a treat, my grandmother made for it a mustard sauce. She put a handful of dry mustard seed in a china wash basin with a pint or so of skimmed milk and a large iron cannon ball which was kept for this special purpose. Seating herself on a stool, she held the basin on her lap, gripping it with her thighs, and then, with a swaying, rocking motion she kept the cannon ball whirling round the inside rim of the basin until it had crushed the mustard seed, which as it amalgamated with the milk, became a paste. As more milk was added it became the sauce. The process lasted hours; she obviously enjoyed her skill controlling the heavy ball. Never once did it sag to the bottom centre nor did it ever shoot over the rim of the basin.

She believed in the efficacy of the old-fashioned nauseating castor oil, and regularly dosed me twice a year, keeping for the purpose a special ruby-coloured wine glass. In it she poured about half an inch of port wine, then from three to four times that quantity of castor oil, then another half inch of port. She explained at length to me the theory that the attractive colour of the glass and the thin layer of sweet port surrounding the large globule of castor oil ought to make the drink very palatable, but the dreadful taste was always there, despite her reasoning.

She had at her command an arsenal of wise saws and terse proverbs, so many of them pregnant with the bitter wisdom characteristic of the folk bred and reared on the stern bleak acres of Buchan. Rarely did a situation arise which she failed to sum up in one devastating epigram. As a rejoinder to implied criticism she had a maxim, 'Bide wi'me and ye'll ken me', meaning that the better she was known the more she would be liked or appreciated. In its undertone of aggressive assurance and confidence this had the arrogance of the Royal motto 'Dieu et mon droit'.

To us youngsters the social event of the long winter was the party given for us at Christmas time by the hotel-keepers—John and Mrs Ritchie. Other parties there were to which, as they were more in the nature of family gatherings, I was not invited, but I did, every year, hope to hear one of the Ritchie boys knock at our door. And, since I was five years old, I had been secretly in love with Polly Ritchie—a year older than myself. Then one year the invitation came when Annie was in an angry mood. She opened the door to the boy's knock and from inside the room I heard the words which meant so much to me. I heard her reply abruptly, 'No, he is not to go', followed by the banging shut of the door. She gave no reason for her attitude. I was so deeply mortified and humiliated that I could have wept, and for weeks avoided meeting any of the Ritchie family lest they might expect some explanation.

The hours I had to spend in school were not happy ones. I had a slow ear and no head for arithmetic, but there was one subject in which I could hold my own with ease—geography. I found I could memorise anything visual and, having studied a map, I could from memory reproduce it accurately and in detail without effort. Great was my astonishment when I saw that none of my schoolmates, all cleverer than I, had the same faculty. This small talent must have impressed even Annie. On one of her visits to Aberdeen she brought back to me a small box of moist watercolours with a camel hair brush. The first use I made of this was to draw and colour a battle-piece of a gaily-tinted Highlander mourning the loss of his companion who lay dead in the middle distance. I tried hard, but with no success, to colour the cannon a light cool grey but had to be content with a dirty-looking brown. It didn't occur to me to put on a very thin wash of black.

Between the village and the sand dunes bordering the sea lay the Udny Links, common ground that formed a natural golf course on which nine greens were kept trim. The course was free to all, and golf was taken so seriously by the grown-ups that it was accepted as the universal antidote to work on six days of the week.

Every boy in the village had his lacerated gutta-percha golf ball and his cleek which served him as driver, iron, mashie, putter and general weapon. My one success was in a competition for boys under twelve years of age where the prizes were a golf club, a pair of live pigeons, and a melon. I won the second prize—the pigeons—which were given me in a sort of wicker case that had to be returned to the prize-donor, a neighbouring farmer. Proudly I nailed together a packing case, cut with my knife an arched hole in the front, and set up my dove-cot on the end wall of the communal garden. Immediately I put the pigeons inside they flew off and I never saw them again.

The golf flags marking the holes on the Links were tall bars of half-inch square iron with two circles of sheet iron rivetted at right angles to the top end. Between school sessions, one sunny noonday, I was on the course with another boy. At the third hole I picked up the heavy flag to replace it in the hole, but I had grasped it too low and the iron swerved, the sharp point piercing my left foot, which was close to the hole, between the tendons of the third and fourth toes. I hastily removed my shoe and stocking, expecting blood. Instead, there was a nice clean red hole through my foot.

Replacing my shoe I limped back to school, imploring my companion to say nothing of this to anyone, as I was terrified at what Annie might say or do if she discovered my shoe had been ruined. In the evening I stole into the neighbouring boat-builders' yard and with a mixture of thick tar and dust stopped up the hole in the sole. In less than a week the hole in my foot had healed to a small red scar, but I walked during that week with the toes of my left foot so curled that they were permanently 'hammered'. My companion proved loyal. The hole in the sole of my shoe was not discovered, although the corresponding hole in the upper was the cause of much conjecture and questioning at home.

Many of my school companions were, I knew, thrashed severely by their parents on occasions of misdemeanour, forgetfulness or stupidity, this being a concomitant recognised as necessary to their proper upbringing. I was no exception. Annie's method was to hit me with her fist on the back of my neck.

Although the necessity for punishing me was usually beyond my understanding, it never occurred to me to question her right to do so until the day when, my foot being still numbed, I tripped on a projecting stone, fell on my face and spilt the contents of a flagon—a pennyworth of milk—which I was bringing home from a nearby farm.

I had at the moment no penny to replace the milk, thus concealing knowledge of my accident, so had to confess the loss. She came towards me, her face contorted with anger. Thoroughly frightened, I backed across the room, and as she still approached threateningly I seized, in desperation, the poker from the fender and prepared to defend myself. She stopped, baffled, and turned away with a 'you just wait' look on her face, but from that day on she never again beat me.

From half way across the Links my schoolmates could read the time on the clock of Holyrood Chapel spire, but at that distance of about half a mile the hands and figures on the dial were, to my eyes, one soft blurr, a circumstance which puzzled and embarrassed me. By the merest chance one day I happened to look through Annie's spectacles. Instantly the whole visible world sprang into tight definition full of fascinating detail.

It dawned on me then that my eyes were not normal like my companions' and that this was how they saw the world and could read the distant time. With some misgiving I told Annie that I could see better through her spectacles than with my own eyes. All she said was, 'Do you want to have to wear glasses like me? Don't you ever touch my glasses again.'

Through the narrow gap in the rampart of sand dunes protecting the land from the sea, the tide rushed in, filling the estuary and making of it a long lake. It poured out on the ebb leaving exposed stretches of mud flats, most of them encrusted with mussels, between which wound the channel. Outside, in the sea, the sandy bar, altered by every gale, made navigation difficult even for the two small steam and one sailing vessel owned locally. Several men engaged in various jobs, but mostly in attending to the salmon stake-nets, were recognised as pilots and they made it their business to know the deep water through the treacherous, shifting bar.

Easterly gales were frequent during the winter. If a rocket, fired from the lifeboat-house a mile distant, exploded above the village it was the signal that a ship was in distress and that every able-bodied person had to drop tool or implement and hurry across the Links to man, or help launch, the lifeboat. The postman left the mail where he was delivering at the moment and the school was closed.

To launch the lifeboat in the river was, as often as not, impossible, as the bar was a mass of curling breakers and the tide running in. The boat on its broad-wheeled carriage might have to be pulled for miles along the coast in soft sand and blowing spray which bit and stung exposed skin. Long ropes were attached to the carriage; everyone lent a hand and the procession pulled itself slowly towards where in the distance a tragic cluster of men clung to a broken mast on a hull slowly being pounded to pieces far out amongst breakers.

The crew of the lifeboat strapped on their cork jackets, took their places, each man with his oar ready. Roped one to the other, men pushed the carriage far out amongst the surf. As the boat slid off the carriage the crew pulled desperately to keep its head to the sea. All watched breathlessly as it alternately disappeared and stood on end as it crested the towering breakers. Hours afterwards the boat returned with the rescued men, its crew exhausted. Only a team of superb seamen could have come back alive from their fight with the storm; they regarded it as all in the day's work and each man drew his allowance of 5s.

Invariably the storm was followed by a clear, calm day. A thin line of wreckage lay at the high-water mark along the coast, encouraging hopes of treasure. The 'tide-watcher'—the local customs officer in his worn uniform—kept a watchful eye on the figures prowling slowly along amongst the fragments of yesterday's fine ship.

My grandmother and I found a Bible, which the tide-watcher allowed us to retain as it was printed in a language no one could read. To my joy I found a cigar-box, empty but redolent of an alluring aromatic odour the like of which I had never smelt.

Every July a Flower Show was held in the village Public Hall. Prizes were offered by various patrons for the best vegetables or fruit or flowers. The village grocer, Willie Murray, offered one year a prize of 2s. 6d. for a drawing of the local antiquity—the ruined keep, Knockhall Castle, built in 1565—with the cautious proviso that the winning drawing 'would become the property of the donor'.

Furtively I studied that ruin until I had memorised it.

At home I got a large sheet of cartridge paper, made the outlines and painstakingly filled in between with as stony-looking stones as I knew how. I knew it would improve it vastly if only I could make one part of the ruin look near and the other recede, but how to do this? The subtleties of perspective and chiaroscuro were unknown to me. Anyway, it was unmistakably Knockhall Castle. Meticulously I printed my name in the bottom corner. Misgivings assailed me as I took it, rolled in a newspaper, to the show. I felt I was exposing myself, naked, to the eyes of a hostile world.

It won the prize. There were no other entries.

When the show opened, there it was pinned on the wall with, on it, an impressive prize label. Apart from the 2*s*. 6*d*. which meant wealth to me, the effect produced was astonishing. Sacrosanct dignitaries of the village who, till now, would not have seen me had they looked my way, graciously bestowed on me words of recognition and congratulation.

I did so hunger for a few words of praise from Annie, but she kept her stoical reserve and gave no indication of pleasure.

School was a daily ordeal and 'home work' a constant bugbear. All of my companions seemed to have elder brothers or parents who explained to them the mysterious workings of equations and guided them amongst the intricacies of Latin tenses and declensions. I had no one to help me and had to stumble along laboriously far behind the average.

In the schoolroom we were seated on forms behind long desks and faced the schoolmaster who stood out on the 'floor' holding in one hand a six-foot wooden 'pointer' as though it were his sceptre and in his other hand his leather 'tawse' like the sword of an executioner.

The order would be given:

'All stand—Back to back and face to face. Take your slates and slate pencil.'

In this position, which was intended to prevent 'copying' from one's neighbour, we were given 'dictation' and 'sums'.

The Shorter Catechism bulked largely in our daily curriculum and took up a considerable part of each forenoon's time. All we boys and girls in age from 11 to 13 would be seated, nervously apprehensive, in a dead silence, each erect and with our arms folded, waiting. The schoolmaster surveyed us with a critical frown, then suddenly fired the question.

'Robert Fullerton, what are the decrees of God?' Robert Fullerton, his arms still folded, shot to his feet as though released by a trigger: 'The decrees of God are his eternal purpose according to the counsel of his will, whereby, for his own glory, he hath foreordained whatsoever comes to pass.' Robert sat down, relieved. The chances were about 8 to 1 against his being asked another question that day. A moment's silence, then,

'William McBeath, did all mankind fall in Adam's first transgression?'

W.McB. 'The covenant being made with Adam, not only for himself, but for his posterity; all mankind, descending from him by ordinary generation, sinned in him, and fell with him in his first transgression.'

'Frank Simpson, what is the misery of that estate whereinto man fell?'

F.S. 'All mankind by their fall, lost communion with God, are under his wrath and curse and so made liable to all miseries in this life, to death itself, and to the pain of hell for ever.'

'John MacIntosh, what is sanctification?'

J.McI. 'Sanctification is an act of God's—'

'Come out to the floor.'

John McIntosh, aged 11, stumbled along behind the backs of the pupils wedged in his row and, standing in front of the schoolmaster, timorously held out his hand to receive on the palm two vicious downward swipes with the leather tawse. With a trembling lip he returned to his seat.

'John Loutit, what is sanctification?'

J.L. 'Sanctification is the work of God's free grace, whereby we are renewed in the whole man after the image of God and are enabled more and more to die unto sin and live unto righteousness.'

'Gordon Rae, what is required in the eighth commandment?'

G.R. 'The eighth commandment requireth the lawful

procuring and furthering the wealth and outward estate of ourselves and others.'

'James Anderson, what is forbidden in the eighth commandment?'

J.A. 'The eighth commandment forbiddeth whatsoever doth or may unjustly hinder our own or our neighbour's wealth or outward estate.'

Although the Shorter Catechism was, as stated on its title-page, 'approved anno 1648, by the General Assembly of the Church of Scotland, to be a Directory for the Catechising such as are of weaker capacity', the answers to its one hundred and seven questions were to us only a farrago of tortuous sentences and knotty words strung into phrases that were difficult to memorise. Each one of us knew that sooner or later we would trip over a misplaced or slipped word and our one concern was to keep ahead, for as long as possible, of that dreaded moment.

Almost every one of us developed an individual nervous affliction. With me it took the form of digging my nails into the joints of my middle fingers; and snipping off with my sharp teeth the roughnesses I thereby raised. The flesh was in a perpetual raw state for years.

After one of the annual 'examinations' a village housewife, surveying us flocking from school, was heard to remark, 'God be thanked that the examination's over and they a' still alive.'

Across the burn from the church lay a large farm. The prosperous tenant's daughter—Nellie Mackenzie—enjoyed a local reputation for her flower pictures—real oil paintings on 'opals' and 'plaques'. She had seen my drawing in the Flower Show and invited me to watch her paint in oils one memorable Saturday.

At last the day dawned. She took me to an upper room filled with a new smell, that of linseed oil, an easel and two chairs. On the easel rested a slab of opaque white glass having a matt surface, and pinned alongside it a chromo-lithograph of a spray of roses. Bright tubes of colour filled a box on a nearby table. Lightly in pencil she drew in the roses, faithfully following the shape of those on the 'copy'. The big moment had come. She stuck her left thumb through a hole in a thin board and from the tubes squeezed out small dollops of white, yellow, red, blue, and green paint. Fascinated, I watched her mix the colours on the palette. What astonished me was that they stayed put where she wanted them on the opal, instead of wandering about like water-colour washes. Her work seemed very detached and patchy until she began to fill in the green foliage, when it 'came together' in a remarkable manner. By the time the daylight faded she had made, it seemed to me, an exact replica of the chrome. Afterwards, at high tea, Mackenzie himself sat at the head of the table and cut slices from a cured ham—a delicacy new to me: altogether an unforgettable day.

Two or three copies of a weekly periodical, the *Boys' Own Paper*, found their way into the village and were bought by whichever of us had pennies to spare. In them appeared in 1895/6 a series of articles, 'A Plain Guide to Oil Painting', by Hume Nisbet. I read those articles until I could almost repeat them from memory. A window had been opened, and through it I saw that outside the village existed a different world—a world in which pictures were regarded seriously. An artist with an odd foreign name—Rembrandt—was invested with a sacred aura and obviously he and possibly many others had been able to earn a livelihood by painting.

The village possessed no paintings as such. The nakedness of parlour walls was relieved by cheap chromo-lithographs, calendars, and vignetted photographic enlargements of members of the family. The acquisition of a painting for the purposes of enjoyment would have been regarded as a bit queer. The day of the cheap reproduction of famous paintings had not yet dawned.

Hume Nisbet's articles kindled an ambition in me which I dared not confess to a living soul, certain and fearful as I was of the caustic jeer. Secretly, I collected pennies and kept my little fund beneath a brick in a wall.

Someday I would have enough to buy a box of oil colours.

A latent jealousy existed between the schoolmasters of Newburgh, Foveran, and Culter-Cullen schools. It became active bi-annually when pupils of the three schools competed for a bursary of £5 annually for three years. Ten or twelve scholars were groomed for the competition by each schoolmaster, and in October 1896 I, aged 12, was one of the competitors from the Newburgh school. I had no hope of winning as, of the four subjects, grammar and composition were obscure and arithmetic an insoluble mystery; in geography alone I had a shy confidence.

When, four months later, our schoolmaster opened the letter of the results in the presence of the assembled scholars and announced I was the winner, he and I were the most dumbfounded of all of us. His two favourite scholars were second and third and, obviously chagrined, he drew attention to the fact that the arithmetic paper was so easy anyone could have done it, adding that, as regards the geography paper, 'James McBey has always, for some reason, been good at that subject.' Annie betrayed appreciation to the extent that she purchased a box of 25 cigars and insisted I present them to him, which I did with the utmost reluctance. Had they been good cigars I would have been even more unwilling.

Next year, when the first instalment of the bursary was paid to me, I hired a cycle and pedalled the thirteen bleak miles south to Aberdeen, bent on buying myself a box of oil colours. The wind, the dust, and the gradients conspired against me but eventually I entered the city.

Although I had been taken to Aberdeen by Annie for a few hours when a child of five, my memories of that occasion were of two interminable dark journeys in a stuffy stage coach, with, between, three hours in a waiting room at the Infirmary. This time I was on my own. The clatter and shrill grind of the iron-shod traffic on the granite setts of the streets deafened me; the merchandise cunningly displayed in the enormous shop windows was a joy to gaze upon, and the exotic smells from the fruiterers so captivated me that I bought four bananas and two tomatoes, neither of which I had ever tasted. At James Stephen & Sons, Woolmanhill, I chose, from a bewildering array of materials, a tinned black enamelled box containing twelve tubes of oil colours, brushes, palette, and bottles of linseed oil and turpentine, costing 7s. 6d., and two canvas-covered boards. The serious attitude which the astute salesman bore towards both me and my purchase was warmly gratifying; I felt I had embarked on a dual life.

Halfway back on the return journey I could resist no longer. I had to see my box. I stood my cycle against a stone dyke, undid the elaborate string arrangement securing it, and feasted my eyes on it and its contents. I peeled the first of my bananas wondering the while from which far-off land it had come. I thought the luscious-looking red tomatoes would be still more delectable, but they held only bitter disappointment.

On one canvas board I painted an old umbrella-mender; on the other a musician blowing a large brass wind instrument, both copies from coloured lithographs in some periodical. My grandmother thought they were wonderful, but Annie was now too blind to see them.

II

I was now nearing 14 years of age and soon I would have to earn a livelihood.

The isolated little farm of East Pitscaff was tenanted by a cousin of my mother—John Torn. John was a natural engineer, compelled by his parents to carry on the farm and scrape a living from the refractory earth for himself and his wife and children. His heart was not in farming but in a heaven he had constructed for himself, a small corrugated iron shed which contained a forge, work bench, guns, wind gauge, batteries, and tools for every conceivable purpose.

The frequent Saturdays I spent with him in this workshop

were high spots in my life. Fascinated, I watched this super-man, eyes dark grey, very deepset; face and head covered with untidy black hair; slow-moving, slow-speaking, choosy of his words, bent over his bench, patiently, intently, and skilfully bringing into the world a child of his brain. He treated me as a valued confidant and assistant and spoke to me as man to man, which flattered me.

I wanted to be an engineer.

Almost cut off from civilisation he was then (1897), making a combustion engine according to his own theories. He was a water-diviner of the first accuracy and derived a quiet enjoyment from the incredulous bewilderment of all. He could not but be aware that he was wasting his talent in that desolate atmosphere, but never did he speak of loneliness or disappointment.

The nearest bank to Newburgh was at the village of Ellon, six miles up the river Ythan. There the North of Scotland Bank had a branch of which James H. Brown, big, bluff and bearded, was agent or manager. He was a personal friend of both my grandmother and Annie and gave serious advice as to the investing of their capital—£600 and £200 respectively. Often on Saturday afternoons he came to Newburgh for a round of golf on the links and usually had tea with us. After one of these visits Annie informed me that he had suggested I should sit for the entrance examination to the bank, to which proposal she had agreed. She added, 'the opportunity is a good one, the work light and clean'.

I had not been consulted. My engineering aspirations I had kept to myself and now they had to vanish. Stern necessity forbade delay and, having no concrete counter-proposal, I had meekly to acquiesce. I saw myself as a complete failure in a bank, but at least Newburgh might not learn of it.

Now that there was a possibility of my going out into the world, Annie had me write to my father (who had left the district and leased the farm of Beddlestead, near Woldingham in Surrey) telling him of my prospects. He wrote back after the lapse of a fortnight:

Dear James, I received your letter some time ago. I am glad you are likely to get into a Bank. If you are successful I will try to help you.

Yours faithfully,
James McBey.

A month later I was summoned to sit for the examination. I cycled to Ellon on the day appointed and had to wait for an hour in the agent's private room until the inspector was disengaged. The furnishing of this room was most unusual, consisting of a huge bookcase filled with books, a large flat leather-topped desk with drawers in it, a pipe-rack holding six or seven worn dirty-looking wooden pipes, and several chairs, two of which were upholstered all over and actually covered with leather.

But what, amid this opulence, drew and held my attention was a small picture, about five inches by nine, hung by itself on the wall. There could be no doubt about it; it was a genuine oil painting—the first serious painting I had ever seen. The subject was an interior with figures illuminated by the light coming from a window on the extreme left. On a label on the frame was printed: 'Scottish Interior' by George Paul Chalmers, R.S.A. The figures seemed to live and the wall forming the background was behind them, not just between them. How could paint be made to do this? It bordered on legerdemain.

Engrossed in this, I had to be summoned several times by the inspector, who questioned me closely about my apparent deafness, testing me meanwhile by the ticking of his watch at various distances. The inspector was slight, baldish, and grey. His movements and speech were measured, quiet, almost stealthy. His small grey, red-rimmed eyes regarded me furtively. He gave me dictation from a newspaper and a long column to add up. These I managed correctly but I felt he disliked me.

A month later the Newburgh butcher, cycling homewards, stopped at the school and handed me a letter from the Ellon banker, informing me I had to commence work in the bank at Aberdeen in two days; that I was to be on trial for two months which would count as the beginning of a five years' apprenticeship; that my salary would be £10 for the first year, rising by £5 annually.

I hurried home and read the letter to Annie and my grandmother. Neither said one word. Minutes passed in silence. I was dumb because, although I loathed the idea of working in a bank, I realised I had to work somewhere, somehow, as, no matter how thriftily we lived, we were eating into our meagre capital. Finally, Annie said to my grandmother, 'Jimmy and I will have to live somewhere in Aberdeen. Are you willing to come with us?'

Hitherto I had taken for granted the daily uneventful round of our lives; only now, suddenly, did I realise that my going out into the world might mean a separation and the break-up of the home. The affection which my grandmother and I had for each other had always been of a furtive nature. Any display, no matter how slight, was resented by Annie who sulked and made the atmosphere unpleasant for days on end. The possibility of being parted from my grandmother, the only friend I had, was a thought that numbed me. She kept on steadily knitting a stocking, not replying to Annie's question, but I noticed her eyes became moist. Never till then had I seen her betray emotion.

I did not dare show how much I wanted her to come with us, but the suspense was becoming more than I could bear. Partly to end it and partly to hint to her how I felt, I offered to contribute all of my £10 salary to help keep the three of us. Annie said, 'It's not much, but we shall have to manage.' At last, my grandmother spoke. 'If you want me I'll come.'

Events had happened so quickly that I had not paused to wonder where she would have lived had she decided against coming with us. She had two married sons, each with young families with whom she would doubtless have been very welcome. Perhaps she still hoped to make our home less miserable.

Next day Annie and I climbed on the bus for Aberdeen. We looked up a Newburgh woman in Urquhart Road—Mrs Argo, a widow with two sons—and it was arranged that I should stay with them for the two months until the term. Annie, at random, took a lease of three rooms at 42 Union Grove, and then purchased for me a grey suit with long trousers, six white dickeys, six pairs of white cuffs, a hard black ugly-looking bowler hat and a pair of shoes.

After I had seen her off on the Newburgh bus at Meal-market Street I returned to my lodgings feeling lost and lonely. My landlady explained at length how the gas jet lighting the room had to be turned off, not blown out like an oil lamp, otherwise we would all be found dead in the morning. It was long before I could sleep that night. I knew that no matter what happened now, I had left the village for ever. To return would be to admit defeat. Only retired sea captains went back and that because they had made their fortunes and, having wandered to many lands and being free to choose, they believed Newburgh was after all the best place on the globe to await the coming of death.

My new toggery lay on a chest beside my bed. The long trousers were symbols of manhood; the hard black hat, the dickeys and the cuffs were the livery of respectability. Tomorrow and possibly for the rest of my life I would have to be inside that armour, designed apparently to constrict and harness the wearer.

The next day, the fifteenth of March 1899, I buttoned myself in my quaint outfit and timidly entered the office of the North of Scotland Bank Ltd, a vast imposing interior of marble, plate glass, brass, and mahogany. Men of all ages were scurrying about bearing papers, books, and bags of coins.

I was ushered into the 'Inspectors' room, where were three inspectors.

First Inspector: 'You are to go to the George Street Branch, Mr McBey. Do you know how to get there?'

My being addressed for the first time in my life as 'Mr' startled me. I had thought that title was reserved for the schoolmaster or the minister.

—'I do not know any of the streets of Aberdeen.'

Second Inspector: 'When addressing an inspector you say 'sir' Mr McBey.'

'All right. I mean Yes, sir.'

First Inspector: 'You go along Union Street till you come to St Nicholas Street. Go right out until you come to the George Street Branch.'

—'I understand; yes, sir.'

First Inspector: 'There you will give this letter of introduction to the agent, Mr Saunders.'

Mr Saunders was a round-headed man, fiftyish, white-haired, baldish, with a thick white moustache, stained a bright yellow in the centre. Red-rimmed bulbous blue eyes projected under thick reddish eyebrows. He asked me about my education and then said:

'Are your parents alive?'

'My mother is.'

'Is your father dead?'

This question floored me. As my father and I had seen one another only once, and then had not exchanged one word, I foresaw complications, so I replied—

'He was a farmer.'

This had the desired effect. Mr Saunders took my use of the past tense as an answer to his question.

'What was the name of his farm?'

'Mains of Foveran.'

Having satisfied himself that my family was of no consequence, he took me to the general office and introduced me to the accountant. The accountant wasted no time. At once, he put me in the charge of the youngest clerk, Mr Greig, who, having served one year, was now being promoted.

For the next twelve months or so, until it became my turn for promotion, I would occupy the position of 'George Street trotter'.

A broad mahogany counter, the two tellers' boxes, and a high obscured glass screen cut the depth of the office in halves and separated the 'front' (for the customers) from the 'back' or workroom of the clerks of whom there were four besides the accountant and the trotter. All the clerks looked alike, clean, drab, and very busy. Everyone was addressed and referred to as Mr This or Mr That. Here was a self-contained world of impersonalities, so different from the kindly familiarity of the village, already ages away.

Mr Greig (indicating the end of one of the high desks standing across the office): 'This is your desk. This is the key. This is the postage book where you write in every letter you post in the right-hand column. If you forget to enter any, or lose stamps and cannot balance you have to make it up from your salary. Here behind you is the copying press. We are late; we'll go and damp the sheets.'

Opening a drawer beneath the press he pulled out a tray in which lay an inch-thick pad of what looked like damp brown paper and a flat brush. He rushed me along a passage to the small chamber which served as toilet, wash- and cloak-room, emptied the tray on the side of the sink, then put the bottom brown sheet back, pasting it into the tray with the wetted brush. 'Now, do the rest just like that, one by one, and don't make them too wet. Then bring them back to me as soon as you can.'

The sheets were of rubberised fabric, very stained. What their purpose was I could not imagine. The cubicle with its obscured glass window, urinal and damp overcoats had a most depressing effect. I was relieved, when finished, to emerge into the purer air of the office.

'Here are the sheets. Are they all right?'

Mr Greig: 'You'll know that when you start copying the letters. Light the candle. Hurry. We have to seal the silver'—indicating fifteen heavy-looking canvas bags which had congregated themselves mysteriously on the floor beside my desk.

'What's in these bags?'

'Silver. £100 in each.'

We dripped blobs of wax where the necks of the bags were tied with the string and pressed on these the brass seal of the Branch.

Mr Greig: 'Now for the cheques for the clearing-house.

We'll have to hurry.' He brought a pile of cheques about two inches thick and showed me how to check the endorsement. The signature on the back had to tally with the name of the payee on the face. If not, the cheque had to be smacked on the back with the 'endorsement guaranteed' rubber stamp and kept separate for the accountant to sign. The cheques were then dealt like playing cards in seven groups according to the different banks; listed, totalled up, and balanced with another clerk's different listing.

Mr Greig: 'Do you know how to use the telephone?'

—'I have never seen one before.'

Off a hook he lifted what looked like a thin black tumbler attached by a twisted string to a box on the wall, put one end to his left ear, turned a handle on the box and said, 'Hello, Central number three five eight.' After a pause, 'Is that Bain's cab office? Send a cab to the George Street Branch of the North of Scotland Bank immediately.'

He then gave me the black tumbler. 'Now put that to your ear, turn the handle and when you hear Central speaking, say "Three five nine off, please".'

I turned the handle, listened, and a wee voice imprisoned in the tumbler did actually say, 'Central speaking'. Summoning all my vocal strength, I shouted into the small hole 'Three five nine off, please.'

Mr Greig jerked himself back as though he had been struck; there was a commotion of running feet, doors were hurriedly opened; the manager, the accountant, and two clerks, all alarmed, crowded the passage. Humbly, Mr Greig explained what had happened. The manager was not amused, so neither were any of the staff.

In the rear of the main office now stood a girl from a nearby baker. In front of her on a stool was a basket of buns and small mutton pies and by her side a can of milk. The pies cost 2*d*. each, the buns 1*d*. and a glass of milk 2*d*. Each of us bought according to what he could afford. No time off was allowed for lunch. We bit into and chewed our buns at the same time as we collected and tied up the bundles of cheques for the daily clearing at 1 p.m.

The cab had now arrived. We loaded into it the bags of silver coin, thrust the cheques into the leather bag, and rattled over the granite streets to the Head Office, where we delivered the silver to a teller, the cheques to a clerk, and dismissed the cab. Mr Greig: 'Now for the clearing-house, we're late.'

The clearing-house was a large room situated above an 'Italian warehouseman' in Market Street where each bank had its own table and chairs. A peculiar smell, pervasive, strong and friendly, filled the room and staircase. I sniffed. 'What's making that strange smell?' Mr Greig: 'The grocer below is roasting coffee.' Back in Newburgh our grocer sold coffee—a thickish black syrup put up in bottles with glass stoppers, labelled 'Curr's Coffee Essence—one dessert spoonful to a cup of hot water', so I asked, 'Why is he roasting coffee?'

Mr Greig: 'God only knows but never you mind about that just now. This chair is the one for the George Street trotter. Sit down and list correctly the cheques as they are dealt to you. Be careful you don't accept any cheques which do not belong to George Street branch. And hurry up. We're late.'

Quickly I began to pencil in the amounts from a pile of cheques in front of me, to which more were being added every minute. Soon I had six columns of thirty-three amounts each, then the flow began to slacken.

Mr Greig: 'Add them up, quick.' I was slow. I had never had to add in such haste. After four columns were added up . . . Mr Greig: 'We must go. We have to be back by 1.45 at the latest.'

We ran down the stairs and rushed all the long mile to the George Street branch. It was cold; sleet had begun to fall and the pavements were slushy and slippery. At last, panting and sweating, we burst into the office. We dumped the pile of cheques on the desk of the ledger clerk who glanced at the clock and immediately began to deal them into three groups. I had to finish adding up the columns of cheques on my lists which took me a long time as the amounts came out differently whenever I re-added or checked a column. Finally I went to Mr Greig. 'Here is the answer.'

Mr Greig: 'Answer? We don't have answers in a bank; we have totals. And you'll have to be quick and in future give it in before you leave the clearing-house. Today, as you were new to the job we'll telephone it to Head Office. The accountant says I can come with you tomorrow again, but after that you'll have to manage on your own.'

Bewildered, I asked why there was such a hurry. Mr Greig: 'Because some of the cheques will have to be returned; No money to pay them. Now I'll show you how to copy the letters.' About thirty of these, all written in longhand, had accumulated on my desk. He laid two letters face up in the opened book, turning over on them a tissue leaf. From the pile of damp rubber sheets he peeled off one and laid it on the tissue, folded on this another tissue, then two letters face down and so on until all the letters were in the book. He then shoved it in the iron press, whirled the handle tight down, counted ten and released the pressure. He opened the book, took out the damp sheets and the letters, and there on the tissues was an exact facsimile of each letter. Some were very blurred.

Mr Greig: 'Your sheets were too wet. If Mr Saunders sees those there'll be a row.'

I: 'Can all letters be copied like that?'

Mr Greig: 'Only if they are written in copying ink. You mustn't use copying ink for anything but letters. Now, address the envelopes and enter them in the postage book, except the ones I pick out.'

I: 'Why are you picking those out?'

Mr Greig: 'Because all letters to addresses within half a mile have to be delivered, to save the Bank the cost of postage.'

The ledger clerk now rushed round and flung on my desk four cheques with the terse remark 'These go back'.

Mr Greig (gathering them up): 'We must take these back to the different banks by 3 p.m.'

I: 'Why?'

Mr Greig: 'On this one the amounts don't agree, and the other three are "refer to drawer".'

I: 'What does that mean?'

Mr Greig: 'The customers have no money left in their accounts.' (Pointing to one of the signatures.) 'That's the Marquis of . . . His cheques are never any good.'

We rushed around Aberdeen returning the cheques to the banks from which they came. Three o'clock was the deadline after which hour the banks could refuse to accept their returned worthless cheques. By 3.30 we were back again. More letters to copy, address, and list in the book.

At 3 p.m. the bank was supposed to close its doors but competition between the banks was so keen that customers ringing the bell up to 3.20 p.m. were allowed in. Many took advantage of this so that after closing time the counter was lined with late-comers and it was often 4 p.m. before the last had gone. About 4.30 or 5 p.m. all the letters had been copied, some of the staff had gone, and Greig and I started to deliver the twelve or fifteen letters within the half-mile radius. We worked our way down to the Post Office, from there to the Head Office where we left the daily returns and the leather bag.

My feet in their hard new shoes were stinging like swollen lumps of red hot metal and my legs felt stiff as though cast in wood. I had to exert a conscious pull every step I took as though my shoes were iron and the paving stones magnetised.

It was close to 6 p.m. when, at last, I reached my lodging. I had been rushed about without a moment's respite for ten hours, and I had eaten only a bun with a glass of milk.

I could not allow Mrs Argo and her sons and daughter to see me in my exhausted condition, so I seated myself on the bottom step of the stairs for twenty minutes or so to recover. When the ache had almost drained itself from my legs, I entered with all the cheerfulness I could summon, and was greeted with, 'Hello, you're very late. We thought you had got lost. We've kept your tea hot, but everything's a bit spoilt. What sort of work is it in a Bank?'

'Very interesting.'

'Pretty easy, I'll bet. You don't have to bother with difficult customers.'

'That's true.'

'What are the hours? Banks close at 3, don't they?'

'Yes, but we have to tidy up after the bank closes.'

The second day was a repetition of the first and the third day was even worse, as I was on my own. Mr Greig had been promoted to the 'appendices' and no longer accompanied me as guide and mentor.

On this day I had to seal, instead of silver, twelve small bags each containing £100 in gold sovereigns and half-sovereigns. It was interesting the way these bags of bullion lay against one another, almost clinging, so different from the hard nobbliness of the bags of silver. No cab or tram fare was allowed for the conveying of them to Head Office and I was advised to carry the heavy consignment by a short cut, which happened to lie through a slum district. Anyone carrying a parcel of twelve hundred gold sovereigns must walk lopsidedly; I hurried along, very conscious of the interested stares of the loiterers standing outside the many pubs on the way.

Each of the clerks owned, in addition to his 'ordinary' and his 'copying' pen, a 'scraper'. He kept this tool sharp as a razor and was very skilled in the use of it. If he made an error when writing or posting he put underneath the page a circular ebony ruler, bent the paper over this and gently scraped out the error, burnishing the resulting dull spot with the bone handle of his scraper. It was hardly possible to detect the alterations unless by holding the page against a strong light, when the scraped area showed as thinner than the surrounding paper. An honest, unconcealed alteration was for some reason frowned upon; the pages of the ledgers looked tidy and spotless.

After a week, nature began to adjust my strength to my load. I began to fit better into the routine of the work and the incessant adding up of amounts became almost mechanical. My walking muscles grew strong, but hurrying over miles of hard stone pavement kept my feet in constant pain.

On 15 May, the Scottish term day, my grandmother and Annie came to Aberdeen and set up house in the rooms the latter had taken when she brought me to the city two months previously. I now had a home and, as best I could, I concealed my daily exhaustion from my grandmother. She may have noticed it, but she did not dare show open sympathy lest she upset Annie, who sat hour after hour immobile and silent.

Annie was now so blind that she could no longer see the objects in the room and knew her exact position only in relation to the daylit window. She could no longer go out alone; every evening at dusk I walked with her a mile or so along one suburban street after another. We did not converse during those outings. She took no interest in my life or my work and we would return home without having exchanged half a dozen words. She discouraged effectively the tentative friendly overtures of the other five families in the house.

My grandmother cooked for the three of us. For breakfast there was porridge, boiled egg, oatcakes and tea; at 5.30 p.m. a 'high tea' with soup or fish or boiled rice.

We were very fortunate as regards health. A benevolent Providence had endowed each of us with the toughest of constitutions; no doctor crossed our threshold. My grandmother had a profound belief in seaweed as a prophylactic. Three times each year a large bowl piled with raw salty dulse stood on the table and from this we helped ourselves day after day until it was finished. Latterly she had difficulty chewing the tough leaves as she lost the more serviceable of her teeth. It was then my job to grip the dulse throughout with the fire tongs which I had previously heated red hot. The wet plum-coloured leaves sizzled and smoked and smelt like a harbour at low tide. When the mass was limp and of a dirty canary colour she ate it with apparent relish.

Eggs were boiled, wiped, and eaten from their shells as nature obviously intended they should be. My grandmother, after finishing an egg, crushed the empty shell together, chewed and swallowed it. She impressed on me she did this 'to cut up any hairs that might be in the stomach'. Myself I shrank from eating the shell, preferring to let my stomach deal with hairs in its own way.

Gradually I learned from the senior clerks that the 'trotter's' job was an unenviable one in every branch and I longed for the first twelve months to pass when there would be a chance of promotion for me. After eleven months the junior teller left for a position on a tea plantation in Ceylon, and all below him were stepped up a desk.

I was now the 'Appendices', after first showing the new trotter his duties. My new job was to memorise forthwith the number of the ledger page of each account, examine all cheques for technical flaws, mark the page (folio number) on each cheque, list them in three large books and total them correctly, making out a return at the end of each day.

My memory became an index of the 450 different accounts, 350 of which were active. I found I was a kind of pilot for the ledger clerk. He had to post all cheques to the accounts of the drawers; speed and accuracy were of the greatest importance, so that he depended largely on each cheque being correctly folioed and arranged in order for him.

His was a great responsibility. The 'good' customers caused him no anxiety, but he had to know from hour to hour how the accounts of the 'shaky' ones stood. As there was no time to keep consulting the ledgers he had to rely on his memory. One single error on his part—dishonouring a cheque when funds happened to be at the account—might have cost the bank thousands of pounds in damages.

His salary was £30 a year.

At the close of each day the totals were collected and the books had to balance. To balance first shot was a rare event. An error, even if only one penny, had to be searched for until found. Depending, as we were, on each other for correct totals, each courted a reputation for reliability; if one's entries and additions were the last to be checked in the pursuit of the elusive discrepancy, one regarded it as a subtle compliment.

One of my Newburgh schoolmates was, I found, in the Union Bank. He had just discovered the Free Library and showed me with pride his ticket. Any householder could get one and borrow a book free for a fortnight. At once I got a card and my grandmother signed it. At the Library the tall glass indexes facing the public passages formed a wall around the shelves of books, and were divided into classifications of which No. 25 was headed 'Fine Arts'. The day I got my ticket I began to live a double life. Although caged in the bank till 4.30 every day except Sunday, the rest of my waking hours were by the Grace of God and the generosity of Andrew Carnegie spent in another world.

I had no one to guide me in my choice of books so I took out No. 1, Section 25, and began to eat my way right through the seven or eight hundred volumes pertaining to the Fine Arts.

At first it was heavy going. Then gradually I climbed through the antiquated, the ponderous, the redundant, to the more modern additions with photographic reproductions. I found I could get the sense of the writing by concentrating on the centre of the page instead of reading along each line, and developed a selective faculty by becoming aware that each volume was written from the author's personal viewpoint, throwing its illumination on a restricted area, like a searchlight. Tentatively I copied in pencil and pen and ink a few of the illustrations, timidly experimenting in perspective and chiaroscuro, and was fascinated by the illusion of relief and recession which the use of these conveyed.

Towards the close of 1900 the Aberdeen Artists Society held an exhibition in the Art Gallery and covered the walls, floor to ceiling, with paintings, all in impressive gold frames. I managed to get a student's season ticket for 2s. and spent every available free minute studying the masterpieces.

The borrowed works included 'The Penance of Eleanor, Duchess of Gloucester' by Edwin A. Abbey, R.A., 'The

Welcome Footsteps' by Marcus Stone, R.A., and 'Caledonia
Stern and Wild' by Peter Graham, R.A. In the place of
honour was hung 'Miss Ellen Terry as Lady Macbeth' by
J. S. Sargent, R.A.

I was amazed to read in the catalogue that 'The Don from
Balgownie' by David Murray, A.R.A., A.R.C.A., was priced
at £1,000 and 'The Ploughboy' by H. H. La Thangue,
A.R.A., £800.

If only I could afford to have a few lessons in drawing
and painting.

I learned that for a nominal sum I could join a night class
at Gray's School of Art. I was told to equip myself with a
large sheet of drawing paper, a dozen paper stumps, soft
black chalk and a pad of chamois leather. In a room where
thirty or so pupils were busy I was given a drawing board
and seated at a small table in front of which, on the wall,
hung a plaster cast of a rosette about two feet square—an
unattractive subject.

I drew in and chalked and rubbed with the stumps and
sweated over my rosette. On his round the teacher glanced
at it and said that I had just begun, that the smallest details
and surface markings had to be meticulously copied. This,
I saw, would take months, even years, if one cared to spend
the time. I took an intense dislike to that rosette; it became
a lion in my path.

In the long narrow classroom about twenty students of
both sexes were deeply engrossed making highly finished
drawings of ornaments similar to my rosette. All appeared
to be strangers to one another and no one had the courage
to break by speech the penetrating oppressive silence per-
vading the room night after night.

At the table on my right sat a pale-skinned, fine-featured,
dark-haired girl of whose close presence I became very
conscious; that on my left was occupied by a young man
with ivory skin, intensely dark eyes and hair, and small
moustache. He had a stiff knee and used a crutch. Neither
of us so much as looked at the other.

We had been working half an hour on the evening of

22 January 1901 when the teacher quietly appeared in the doorway and announced that word had just come that Her Majesty Queen Victoria had died at Osborne, Isle of Wight, and that all classes were dismissed until further notice.

The lame student addressed me in sepulchral tones, 'Well, this is the end of everything.' I was taken aback. It was the first time I had been addressed conversationally by a stranger, and the remark was the first unnecessary one made, so far as I had heard, in that classroom.

For many months the Boer War had been the big theme in the Press, and we were duped into the belief that the British defeats in South Africa were wholly due to the Boers' dirty fighting ways. They wore a uniform the colour of the surrounding veldt and shot our gallant soldiers from behind rocks, bushes and other places of concealment, altogether different from the natives of Egypt, Benin, Zululand, Ashanti etc., who, armed with spears, assegais, and flintlocks, waited bravely in a bunch to be shot or hacked to pieces by recognised cavalry charges.

The serious illness of the Queen—the symbol of over sixty years of successful 'punitive expeditions' and conquest in every quarter of the globe—had temporarily ousted the war progress from first place and was being played up by the newspapers as a national catastrophe fraught with unimaginable peril to the Empire. A subdued hush had lain over all activities for days and now that the unbelievable calamity had happened, the lame student's terse summing-up seemed a puerile understatement.

I baldly agreed with him and together we walked up dark sleety Union Street in silence. His name I learned was Henry J. Rennie.

The bank hung up black-edged cards intimating that they would be closed on the day of the Queen's funeral, the 25th of January.

Copying the detail of that plaster rosette was getting me nowhere and here, unexpectedly, was a free day. I beseeched my grandmother to sit for me so I could try my hand at a portrait. She was coy but, conquering her self-consciousness, agreed to humour me.

On the day of the funeral I was all ready with a real canvas 20″ × 24″ fastened to an easel of three gardeners' bamboos tied tripod-fashion.

She wore habitually a grey Shetland shawl around her shoulders and a white linen 'mutch', a close-fitting cap covering the head and ears, held tight by strings tied beneath the chin and leaving only the face exposed.

She had, carefully stowed away against a special occasion, a black lace mutch. The special occasion had never to my knowledge materialised but she did want to wear it for her portrait. She was obviously disappointed that I chose to paint her wearing the white mutch and the homely Shetland shawl.

During the three hours of the sitting her expression was one of amused, slightly perplexed, benign tolerance. I did try so hard to capture this.

It was a day of snow and sleet. Before 3 p.m. the day-light failed, but I had progressed. When I stood back and regarded my canvas from a distance it looked good. My grandmother's first reaction, when she saw it, was one of complete bewilderment. Anxiously I waited for her words. Then 'It is as good as a photograph.' Only once before in her life, about forty years previously, had she been photographed. Higher praise she could not give.

Annie showed no interest at the time. Several days later a neighbour saw the portrait by chance and exclaimed in amazement at the likeness. An hour afterwards I found Annie standing in front of it as though looking at it. Sadly she spoke. 'I wish I could see it.'

Never before had I heard her refer to her blindness, even indirectly, except in terms of bitterness. I had a spasm of intense sympathy; it seemed that a wall which had always stood between us had fallen down. Before I could free the words which had jammed themselves in my throat, Annie, immediately regretting and con-trolling her momentary emotion, added, 'I hope this is not going to take your attention off your work in the bank'.

The wall was still there.

My portrait became the talk of the tenement. Neighbours asked to see it and made a fuss of it, so much so that Annie, probably slightly jealous, wanted me to paint her also. I did my best, but she made difficulties. For one thing she insisted on a profile, although I assured her that her eyes were perfectly normal in appearance.

Our landlady Mrs Ross called twice a year to collect her rent. When she saw my two portraits she wanted me to paint a full length of her eight-year-old daughter for £5.

For her portrait the child wore a white silk dress hanging in loose vertical folds from the smocking across her chest. The rendering of these loose diaphanous folds, altering their forms with the slightest movement of the subject, nearly drove me crazy.

Mrs Ross was very satisfied with the portrait and had a frame gilt with real gold made for it. My struggle with the silk dress showed me how much I had to learn in the technique of oils. Where could I find someone willing to instruct me?

Opportunely, an advertisement appeared in the evening paper. 'John A. Hay, Artist, 115 Union Street. Lessons in drawing and painting. £1. 1s. 0d. per quarter.'

I pointed out to Annie that as I had earned £5—equivalent to four months of my salary at the bank—by painting Mrs Ross's girl's portrait, it would be money well spent if I had tuition in painting. I then read to her the advertisement, and she offered no opposition.

John A. Hay was in his fifties, thin and lanky. He moved with timidity and deference. He had gentle dreamy blue eyes, thin hair and a wispy moustache, both of a sandy colour, and a soft shy voice. Mildly curious to know why I, working in a bank, should want to paint, he took my guinea and enrolled me as a pupil in his evening class, telling me to come provided with paints, canvas, and a 'copy'. The latter could be rented from an art shop for 2d. a week.

At Stephens's shop, from a pile of hundreds of oleographs, mostly of sprays of flowers without visible supports, I chose as my copy a mountainous woody coast scene with houses perched precariously on a cliff above the bluest of calm seas. It was labelled 'Amalfi'. I thought John A. Hay seemed slightly amused when I appeared with this subject. The room was crowded with young women students, all pupil teachers and all engrossed in painting flowers on opals or art plaques.

John A. Hay installed me in a corner, setting up my canvas and copy on an easel and instructing me to draw in my subject carefully with charcoal. He went the round of his pupils criticising in a whisper. He came to me last, found my drawing satisfactory, and instructed me how to arrange the colours on my palette for painting at the next lesson.

Next night I went ahead on my own and finished the painting. When finally he reached me he looked long at my canvas and then said, 'Where did you say you worked?'

'In the North of Scotland Bank.'

'Have you had painting lessons before?'

'No.'

'You have done that well. Better bring another copy next night.'

At Stephens I chose the only figure subject in the whole collection of copies. It was the head and shoulders of an olive-skinned, dark-haired damsel wearing a black lace mantilla. Her large brown eyes were filled with an expression of intense tragedy. She was labelled 'A Modern Madonna'.

The gentle John A. Hay was genuinely startled when he saw what I had chosen. 'You are (a hesitating pause) ambitious. Well, just draw it in carefully and paint it as you did the landscape.' I detected furtive smiles on the faces of the women students (I was the only male) and I was glad to be in a corner behind the protection of my easel.

John A. Hay did not reach me the first night I worked at my madonna. The next night I finished it and awaited his coming and criticism. At last he stood behind me, silent. He reached over my shoulder, took my painting and showed it to each of the other students in turn. What he whispered to them about it I could not hear. Returning, he set it on my easel and said, 'I want you to stay behind the others. I want to have a word with you privately.'

When we were alone he went to his bureau, fussed a little amongst papers, then crossed the room and handed me an envelope, saying, 'I am returning your money. I can teach you nothing. You will only waste your time by coming here again.' His generous act so surprised me that I left without thanking him. A bridge to freedom had collapsed and I had been left desolate and abandoned.

At home, when, with misgiving, I related what had happened, Annie was puzzled but she made it plain that now she was sure her unsympathetic attitude towards my ambition to paint was justified; that what talent I had led nowhere.

With my fellow clerks in the bank I had little in common. Keenly sensitive to inevitable ridicule, I kept secret my aspirings to the world of art.

Occasionally, in the day's grim hurry, patches of conversation could be sandwiched; unfailingly the subject became that of 'girls', and vague and sketchy tales of conquest were exchanged. The girl secretaries who came to the bank on the business of their firms exuded an attraction apparent throughout the office for as long as they were at the counter. The 'correspondence' clerk—jolly, dark, curly-haired, rosy-cheeked—confided to me regularly every Monday morning. 'Picked up a fine girl yesterday; got all I wanted from her.' Painfully shy and gauche, I could not have talked to a girl had I had the chance to meet one. I envied him his bold handling of sex.

III

Steering a definite course amongst the six or seven hundred volumes comprising the art section in the Library was like crossing a trackless stretch of moorland and morass with no visible landmarks and having to rely on a confusion of directions.

In many ponderous volumes John Ruskin had enunciated his art formulae, deciding authoritatively between the true and the false. The taste of the period was based on what he endorsed. His command of language exercised a spell on me until the day I opened a book with the piquant title *The Gentle Art of Making Enemies* by an artist James A. McNeill Whistler. From that day Ruskin was, for me, a dead Goliath.

R. A. M. Stevenson's *Velasquez* was in such demand at the Library that, badly as I could afford it, I purchased a copy for myself. It cost me 5s. and to get it I had to go without my glass of milk at lunch time for six weeks. One evening in the summer of 1902 I carried home *A Treatise on Etching* by Maxime Lalanne.

Frequently in the course of my reading, etchings had been mentioned, but how they were produced was a mystery to me. I believed it was an elaborate means for the reproduction of paintings (which to a large extent it was before being supplanted by the photogravure process).

Lelanne's *Treatise* was copiously illustrated by actual prints from his own original plates. These were small in size but they conjured up the subjects to an amazing extent. Some of them were elaborately cross-hatched; in others the magical effects were got by frank and sparing use of line, unlike anything I had so far seen. The fullest directions were given as to how to take a sheet of copper, coat it with a film of wax, blacken the wax, draw in the subject with a needle, place the whole in an acid bath, remove the copper frequently so as to paint out with wax the fainter lines, clean off the wax when the acid had done its work, ink the plate, wipe it and press damp paper on it.

The outfit required was an elaborate one, but I felt it was within my power to make one etching by using substitutes. I foresaw the greatest obstacle would lie in the printing, for which a special press was necessary.

Etching had one advantage; it did not necessitate the carrying about of bulky gear. I had not dared to sketch or paint out-of-doors. For a junior bank clerk to be seen with a sketching outfit in the streets would be, I knew well, certain to arouse the derision of my fellow clerks and would be regarded with at least suspicious curiosity by the higher officers of the bank, should it ever come to their knowledge.

All those belonging to the parochial banking world in which I was enmeshed were intensely preoccupied with the grim business of survival on their meagre salaries. They had their own shrewd and canny standards, and viewed with slight tolerance and vinegary scorn anyone indulging in unremunerative activity. To spend time and energy on the study or practice of art was considered as frivolous—the diversion of a trifler. Consequently, I went about the making of my first etching with all secrecy.

From the plumber Blaikie I bought a sheet of 18 gauge copper $4'' \times 5^{1}4''$. With a file I made the edges true and put a bevel all round, finishing and polishing one side with fine emery cloth. Closely following Lalanne's directions I heated the plate and dabbed on the wax ground. After being blackened in the smoke of a candle it cooled to a fine matt surface. To protect this from accidental scratches whilst in my pocket, I covered it with a piece of cardboard to which I had fastened with thread a thick layer of cotton wool as a cushion.

On a sunny Saturday afternoon of July 1902, in a state of suppressed excitement, with a small mirror, my plate and two darning needles in my pocket, I walked down to the harbour, to the quay where the Shetland steamers tied up. This quay, known as Point Law, formed the tip of a tongue of land dividing the harbour into two arms of water. In the easternmost of these was tied up a fleet of herring boats, most of them of the 'Zulu' type, each with two tall pole masts and lug sails.

I picked a deserted part of the quay where were piled big wooden packing cases. Sticking my penknife in one of them I hung my small mirror on it, so that, standing with my back to the fishing boats, I could see them reflected in the mirror.

Minutes passed before I had the courage to make a single line on the black matt surface. One contingency I had not foreseen: intense concentration made me involuntarily hold my breath; my pulse pounded so that I could not control the hammer-like motions of my hands, the impulses of which, although slight, would be sure to record themselves immediately my needle touched the wax.

I waited, trying to relax. I kept reminding myself that, although a mistake was difficult to cover up or rectify, the plate, as an object of expense, was not thereby spoilt; that I could wash off everything with turpentine. Gradually I became more controlled and once started I gained confidence.

The ease with which the needle, as it touched the black wax surface, made a copper-coloured line was almost uncanny. Eventually I finished, rewrapped my plate with care, walked home in a state of suspended elation, and straightaway immersed it in a bath of half nitric acid and half water.

Everything happened according to Lalanne, whose treatise I had handy, open at the page.

Bubbles grew on the copper-coloured lines. I took them off gently with a feather. Several times I removed the plate from the acid and painted out the lines where I wanted distance, trying to guess the depth of the lines by the feel of the needle in them. It was a messy-looking object by the time I decided to remove the wax coating. Turpentine and a wipe cleaned this off and suddenly there was my drawing in black lines on the copper. It was astonishing. But how was I to get a print?

So far as I knew, there was not in the whole of Aberdeen a copperplate press like the one Lalanne described. This was an elaborate affair, but the principle was simple—a very powerful squeeze.

It was just possible that the copying press in the bank would do the job. Surreptitiously I took my plate and the few accessories necessary and tried it. Nothing happened.

The pressure obviously was too dissipated. It was mortifying to be defeated so near to my goal.

A week later it suddenly occurred to me that our mangle in the basement might be made to do the job. It had strong wooden rollers. If the top one were screwed down tight the spring pressure might be just sufficient.

I cut a piece of thick linoleum for a travelling plank and ran it a little way between the rollers. On it I placed my copper plate, inked and wiped; then the dampened paper; then three pieces of blanket. I screwed down the pressure all it would take and slowly turned the handles till the blankets were clear at the other side of the rollers.

Gently I peeled off the blankets and the paper. There, in front of my unbelieving eyes, was a perfect print.

There was a touch of the miraculous about it, like taking a hole in one at golf. To make certain it was not an absolute fluke, I pulled two more prints. Both came out as good as the first one.

I purchased two more copper plates. On one I drew a quick impression of three boys looking over the edge of a quay at their fishing line, and on the other a portrait of my grandmother. Attaching no value to these prints, I gave several to co-tenants who flattered me by asking for copies.

My use of the family mangle had its disadvantages, chief of which was the poor lighting of the basement where it stood, necessitating the inking and wiping of my plates by the light of an oil lamp.

When prowling through a junk yard I came upon what appeared to be the discarded steel piston rod of a marine engine. If this could be cut in two and suitably turned it might form the rollers of a press.

My uncle George Gillespie had not succeeded in making a paying concern of the smithy at Newburgh which he had inherited from my grandfather, and had come to Aberdeen with his family, renting a blacksmith's shop within a mile of my home.

He could work wonders with a hammer and a bar of red hot iron so I consulted him as to the feasibility of making a press. He was willing to try but as he had no turning lathe he stipulated I had to supply the rollers, and to help him at the forge. I made full-scale drawings of the component parts and bargained with the junk yard to have the thick steel rod cut in two and turned according to my drawing.

George and I worked many evenings of the winter of 1902/3 constructing that small press. It was, when finished, a powerful machine, and although the rollers were only $2\frac{1}{2}$ inches in diameter, it functioned perfectly so long as it was not asked to take large plates.

The satisfaction I had with my little press was tempered by Annie's attitude—a strangely hostile one. Frequently she had indicated that it was in my own interest to give my whole attention to my work in the bank, although she had no reason to think that I was neglecting my duties. The crisis came when she flatly forbade me to bring my press home, saying there was no space for it in the house.

Our tenement consisted of three rooms—a combined kitchen and living-room, a bedroom, and a parlour; the two former were in constant use but the parlour was a chamber sparsely furnished with the more varnished and costly of our household goods and sacrosanct for the formal reception and entertainment of 'visitors'. In our particular circumstances there had not ever been occasion to use the parlour; and as there were two low, wide, built-in empty bookshelves, I felt Annie's reason was unjust, as my press was a small affair, at the most 24 inches by 14 by 9.

Clearly this was to be the show-down between Annie and myself. Either I had to submit meekly to her fiat and abandon every aspiration I had harboured or make a determined stand and establish a relationship between us so definite that I would be free of her constant discouragement and gibes.

Deep in my mind I had secretly nursed the dream that if I could but make a success, no matter how small, of my painting or etching it might prove to be the avenue of escape from the interminable daily grind of the bank machine. For me the future, on the terms offered by the bank and by Annie, was not worth facing, so I made up my mind to bring home my press and defy her. And besides, it was my grandmother's capital which was our main support. The tenement was in her name, and she, I suspected, had a secret belief in me.

Quietly and furtively I brought the different parts of my press into the parlour and put it together on the top of the low bookcase. On its travelling plank I stood my bottle of nitric acid.

In the kitchen Annie was seated in the chair she always occupied; her face was grim and her almost sightless eyes unfocused. Quietly I intimated that my press was in the next room, on the top of the bookshelf next to the window, that I intended it should stay there and, as a precaution, I had balanced on it a bottle of strong acid which if upset would break and completely destroy the carpet and possibly set the house on fire.

The statement was drastic; it had to be. If in her mind there lurked any doubt as to my resolve she was, I knew, capable of unscrewing and concealing or throwing out of the window vital parts of the machine. She could approach it only by touch, not by sight, and the balanced bottle of acid would keep her from meddling. Her expression did not change at my words nor did she break the long stony silence which followed.

For weeks thereafter we three lived in the atmosphere of gloomy neutrality engendered by the clash; Annie made no attempt to damage my press and evidently came to accept its presence in the parlour as unavoidable.

I had become so accustomed to the routine of the work in the bank that I could dismiss all thought of it from my mind the moment I pulled the door shut behind me. In a latitude so far north as Aberdeen the summer daylight stretches far into the evening, and it became a habit of mine to wander about the city and the harbour with a prepared copper plate in my pocket. Often, faced with an inspiring subject, I had to hesitate and move on because, although I was now earning a salary of £30 a year, I had to help towards household expenses; I had few shillings to spare and the cost of the copper plate loomed large in my rigid economy.

In one of the Library's books on Whistler it was related how he searched for and used old paper for the printing of his etchings. Anxious to experiment, I enquired of the second-hand booksellers with no success, but eventually found in the gallery of the New Market a store packed to the ceiling with old books, and kept by a little old man who had tunnelled out for himself a sort of lair amongst them.

He sold me at a penny each blank fly leaves from the books forming the lining of his lair, these being the only ones that could be handled without vast trouble. He informed me that over 90 per cent of his stock consisted of theological works, nearly all of them printed in Scotland during the eighteenth century, and that he purchased them from all over the northern part of the country at a fixed price of 10s. per ton. His replies became evasive when, from curiosity, I asked him about their probable fate.

IV

Every year each clerk had a fortnight's holiday. My holidays for the past four years had been spent at home. There was nowhere I could go without incurring expense that I well knew we could not afford.

This year (1903) I, being now one of the senior clerks, was fortunate enough to get my holiday allotted for the month of July. Unaccountably, in June, my mother insisted that I write to distant relatives in Portsoy suggesting they invite me to stay with them for the fortnight, giving as her reason that she was sure they were well-off and could afford to have me. I had never heard of those relatives and was all against becoming a supplicant. Nevertheless she was stubborn about this and kept alluding to it, so finally I agreed to write in her name, she to sign the letter as well as she could.

The upshot was that I was invited to Portsoy.

I looked forward to this future fortnight and dreaded lest King Edward VII's illness and operation would upset everything. All went as planned, however, and I set out in a state of elated anticipation, tempered by a few qualms. I had never made a journey of such length (all of 60 miles); I had never been in a railway carriage till then, and to crown all I had never before had to fill the role of a guest; here was I about to enter a household of strangers.

Instead of having to ask my way when I arrived at the station, I was actually met by one of my host's sons, a lad of 16 who volunteered to carry my bag. This I did not allow as my Gladstone, though tiny, was deceptively heavy, containing, as it did, several copper plates and etching tools, the presence of which I hoped to avoid disclosing, at any rate at first.

My host, Adam Gillan, rented the salmon fishings for miles to the east and west of the coast town of Portsoy and was apparently a man of great wealth and importance.

His house, of impressive size, stood in a commanding position. The large garden, sloping towards the harbour, had in its centre a tall flagpole with a yard from which the Union Jack flew lazily. On the ground floor were a drawing-room, a study, and a real dining-room. Upstairs were what appeared to be innumerable bedroom doors and, of all things, a bathroom. On the floors were carpets and rugs, not linoleum.

To me, accustomed to the most frugal fare, the Gillan meals were impressively sumptuous. A vase of flowers was in the centre of the dining table and a maid in a white cap and apron kept removing the used plates. My host and hostess, their one daughter and four sons, seemed on the best of terms with one another and requests for second helpings caused no embarrassment.

The array of eating implements set at my place—different-sized knives and forks and spoons—disconcerted me at first, but I cautiously watched the others and based my technique on theirs.

Throughout the season my host employed regularly five men whose daily work was to row out in a cobble, extract the salmon from the nets, and despatch them to London boxed in layers of ice. Each net consisted of a 'leader' and a bag or trap at the seaward end, all suspended from corks floating on the surface, the leader forming a sort of fence stretching out from the rocky shore for about 100 yards.

With diffidence I began to sketch in pencil the fisher-men at work, gaining confidence as their reaction was one of amused interest. I used all the copper plates I took with me to Portsoy; four of them survived the sub-sequent acid bath.

My fortnight's sojourn under another roof brought vividly to my consciousness the atmosphere of gloom and depression and antagonism permeating my own home. I tried to analyse it, wondering in my mind if I were to blame and if so to what extent.

Comparison of the two households was impossible. I just did not know where to begin. Annie's whole attitude was anti-social and definitely antagonistic to me.

One time I tentatively indicated that I would like to bring someone to see the portrait I had painted of my grandmother. At once Annie became alarmed and angry and forbade me to bring any stranger into the house. Her apprehension was so genuine and her threats so intense that I never again suggested doing so.

Her hostile attitude inhibited me; I had to suppress and keep secret my hunger for human friendship. By making a definite stand I had won concessions, but these were all of a minor nature and all within our small domestic orbit. I kept myself in the belief that none of my fellow clerks had any inkling of the life I led at home, and wrapped myself in an aloof pretence knowing I could not meet them on the same terms as they met one another. Confronted by an occasional friendly overture I hinted that my mother was an invalid and could see no one.

As each clerk in the bank finished his apprenticeship he was shifted to another branch or accepted a position abroad. I had been promoted from the appendices to the correspondence desk, then to cash book.

Rents and dividends and accounts were paid in May

and November and the bank's books were balanced in September. The work for about ten days in each of these three months was increased to such an extent that the whole staff, with the exception of the manager, had to work late, sometimes till midnight, for days on end.

It was exhausting work for which we got no extra pay; when daylight went the lighting was none too good and we all felt the strain on our eyesight. The office was lit by incandescent gas lamps fixed on chandeliers high above the desks.

The manager with his family lived, rent free, in the house above the bank. An allowance—an ample one of £16 per annum—was granted by the Head Office for gas consumed in the office and in the manager's house above, there being only one meter for the whole building. On nights when we worked late, it was the manager's habit to stand at the rear of the office, betraying anxious impatience by every indication short of words.

The moment a clerk closed his ledger, the old man rushed forward, climbed up on the clerk's high desk and, balancing himself precariously, turned off the gas jet immediately above, thereby gaining a penny or two for himself but at the same time making the light even more dim for the clerks who were still working. This petty performance on the part of our boss, who never under any circumstances departed from his attitude of god-like aloofness and had no interest in any of us except as automatons, aroused our secret amusement.

Frequently we conspired together in that, so far as was possible without arousing suspicion, we should all finish work about the same time. Although we might have been working at full pressure for fourteen or fifteen hours without a break, we were not too exhausted to enjoy thoroughly his exhibition of agility on those occasions.

In 1903 I had been promoted to ledger clerk in the George Street office of the bank. The accounts of the four hundred or so customers were kept in three ponderous ledgers and it was the ledger clerk's job to 'post' the payments and the cheques into the individual accounts. He had to memorise the state of each customer's account and know approximately its constantly changing balance without having to consult the ledger, for which there was no time.

But about thirty or forty clients were in a state of semi-insolvency, some of them overdrawn against securities. All cheques had to be passed by the ledger clerk, who put his initials on a top corner, thus accepting responsibility. He had to maintain an unceasing watchfulness in regard to the thirty or forty shaky customers, whose cheques had to be passed by the manager himself. When one of those cheques was presented the procedure was for the ledger clerk to calculate very carefully how much it would overdraw the customer's account, take the cheque to the manager in his room, give him the exact balance overdrawn and have him initial the cheque.

This particular work soon became routine for me until one day I got a shock. I had taken a wad of doubtful cheques to the manager and as I read off the various overdrawn amounts he initialled several which I knew he should not have passed. His mind was obviously absent. To make certain he had heard me correctly I pointedly drew his attention to the unprecedented overdrafts. He started as though awoken from sleep, pulled himself together, crossed out his initials and told me to dishonour the cheques.

Always after that incident I used ink instead of pencil on the sheet off which I gave him the amounts and those sheets I kept for weeks. I was well aware that were he, absent-mindedly, to initial cheques which, had his mind been functioning normally, he would have dishonoured, it would be his word against mine regarding the amounts I had given him.

Without influential friends or relations in the bank I was, I knew, a natural scapegoat, and it behoved me to protect myself by such cunning as I could muster. I was beginning to stand on my own feet and learning to accept life on the only terms it seemed to offer—that nothing was to be given me, but that much could be mine were I bold enough to demand it and unscrupulous enough to take it.

The lame student who, years before, had spoken to me on the night of Queen Victoria's death, had become my closest friend. He lived nearby; every Sunday afternoon it had been our habit to meet for a long walk of three or four hours. These outings started from and ended at the house of his parents, I being unable, because of Annie, to invite him to my home; never did he attempt to discuss, or betray any inquisitiveness about, my domestic set-up. How much he surmised I did not know; gradually over the course of years I relaxed into a feeling of security that I had with no one else.

What may have fostered a tacit understanding between us was his physical handicap (he had to use a crutch) and my spiritual one. He was three years older than I, deeply religious, widely read, and of a studious and argumentative nature. He upheld all that was settled, established, and orthodox. I learned much from him about the wherefore of many subjects about which, due to my lack of education and my very restricted reading, I felt painfully ignorant for one of my years.

Invariably, no matter what topic engaged our minds when we set out, the discussion eventually came around to theology—a subject which interested us vitally. We argued about the inter-denominational rivalry between the Churches, the hypocritical religious manifestations of the shrewd Aberdonians, the reasons for the universal belief in a hereafter, the problematic divinity of Jesus, the emphasis on the virgin birth and the miracles, what constituted sin, the status of the Jews and the heathen in relation to the doctrine of St Paul, the hanging of battle trophies in Christian churches and many other grave problems, superstitions, anomalies and anachronisms.

Sceptical by nature, I was searching for an unassailable belief—a faith to which I could adhere and which would carry me through life, come what may.

On the termination of my apprenticeship in March 1904 I was transferred to the inspection department at Head Office, where I had to check the interest paid out on deposits by the fifty-odd branches—a sort of policeman's job. This, I found, was just to keep me apparently busy, my real job being to hold myself prepared to go immediately to any of the Bank's branches in Scotland, to take the place of any official who through illness or for other reason had to vacate his post. At Head Office were three of us all holding ourselves in readiness to 'relieve'.

Before many days had passed John Hutcheon, an inspector, stood casually in front of us and said, 'Stephen, the accountant at Kirkcaldy, has to undergo an operation. One of you will have to go immediately and take his place', adding facetiously, 'Now don't all speak at once.'

Kirkcaldy, I remembered quickly, was far away in the Kingdom of Fife but just across the Firth of Forth from Edinburgh where a fine collection of Whistler's paintings was then on exhibition. Here was my chance. Before any of the others could speak I said, 'I'll go, sir'.

The inspector looked surprised, then, 'There is a train in an hour. I'll telegraph Stephen you are taking over.'

Before I left the office I learned why the inspector looked surprised. The Kirkcaldy office was a 'snag'; it had recently been opened; the managers were lawyers who had been chosen for their influence in the town, knew nothing about and were not interested in banking, and the staff was comprised of two very young inexperienced clerks, besides the accountant whose place I was to fill.

Stephen, looking ill, greeted me at Kirkcaldy station with the words, 'Are you Mr McBey from Head Office?'

'Yes.'

(A long pause and survey.) 'How long is it since your apprenticeship was up?'

'Eight days.'

'I did expect they would have sent an experienced man. However that's their affair. You'll find that you will have to take full responsibility. I'm going north tomorrow morning. You can have my lodgings. We'll have high tea, then we'll go to the office where you can take over the cash whilst I go to some friends and bid them goodbye.'

Darkness had fallen by the time we reached the office, which was in the crowded main street. The door was flanked by two long low horizontal windows with wire screening the lower half. Inside, parallel to the windows, ran a long counter, having at the very end a small high glass-screened desk.

The back of the office opened on to a large room, empty of furniture except for a massive safe against one wall. This Mr Stephen unlocked and between us we carried and deposited on the front office counter the cash, about £12,000, which I was now to count and be responsible for so long as I was in charge of the office. A considerable proportion of the cash consisted of £1 notes, tied in bundles of 20. When the lot was piled on the counter it made a bulky show and aroused, I could see, great interest amongst the crowd outside, who, when the electric lights were switched on in the office, had a fine view of the interior through the wire screens. I doubted the wisdom of exposing such a pile of money to the gaze of possible robbers but kept my thoughts to myself.

Mr Stephen, saying he would return before midnight, left me counting the cash. Behind him I promptly fastened the street door on the inside. The street noises outside gradually died away and an uncomfortable silence fell. I knew I was alone in the whole building which was all offices, and I was aware that I was being watched by several shadowy loiterers from the dark street.

I had counted the gold and the silver and most of the notes when, in search of a piece of string, I began groping amongst the contents of the desk at the end of the counter. Suddenly the lights went out and I was left in a pitch-black silence. Not daring to move I waited for the attack, imagining all the forms it might take.

Minutes passed and nothing happened. Silently I felt my way along the counter to where there was a 2-foot ebony ruler. With this as a potential weapon I felt safer. Still nothing happened. I felt my way to the switches, but they were all on. When withdrawing my arm the cuff of my over-coat caught in something and all the lights went on again. I found that the lid of the desk, when lifted, silently touched off a master switch.

When the accountant returned at 1 a.m. he regarded my fright lightly, but I thought to myself that it was well for him he did not come half an hour earlier and enter the office by a back door. I would not even have challenged an intruder.

The next morning he left and I was in full control of the bank. The managers did not bother to appear. I was very nervous, but fortunately nothing untoward happened. The day being Saturday, we closed at midday. I took the earliest afternoon train to Edinburgh and in a state of eager anticipation hurried along Princes Street to the Royal Scottish Academy Galleries.

At first sight the Whistler paintings seemed slightly disappointing. I had imagined a forceful realism and was unprepared for the flat muted lighting, the fastidious silhouette, the softened edges and the restrained colour. Once I got accustomed to this I began to appreciate the masterly simplicity of the compositions.

What fascinated me most of all was the technique. With consummate skill the paint was put on the canvas, the grain of which showed everywhere, in thin semi-transparent layers. Although the brushwork was vigorous, the finished surface had a beautiful enamel-like quality which by comparison made the work of other artists appear rough, forced, even haphazard. Closing-time cut short my study and I returned to Kirkcaldy determined to return every Saturday I could get away.

I had to remain in charge of the bank in Kirkcaldy for six weeks. I was lucky in that only once during the period did a problem arise which had me worried. One of the lawyers who acted as manager was out till 4 p.m.; no one knew where he had gone. His partner—an oldish man—was at his home, indisposed.

Through the clearing house came a cheque for £250 drawn by one of the bank's customers who lived at a distance and had only £45 at the credit of his account. I knew nothing of this person's financial standing nor did either of the two young apprentices, one of whom I sent post haste to get the ailing manager's authorisation for this overdraft of £205. The lad brought back word that the manager was asleep and too ill to be bothered.

The bank had no telephone. By 3 p.m. a decision had to be made and it was now 2.40 p.m. Sorely perplexed, I bethought myself of the friendly accountant of a rival bank. I went to see him—a most unethical procedure—and learned that the drawer of the cheque was quite wealthy. I passed the cheque on my own responsibility and was tremendously relieved when £250 was paid in by the customer half an hour after the bank closed for the day.

I had been back in the Head Office in Aberdeen less than a fortnight when I was given the chance of a job on a tea plantation in Ceylon at the salary of £300 per annum. I had no desire to go abroad but, as I was earning only £55 in my present position with little prospect of advancement, the salary offered seemed high.

When I told Annie of this opportunity she listened in silence. Without asking me what I thought, she assumed that I wanted to go and after several minutes said, 'What is to become of me, if you go off?' I said that I had not decided to take the position but that we ought to talk it over, as it might be possible for me to remit home a proportion of my salary considerably in excess of what I would ever get in the bank. I could not help adding that, as there never had been any affection between us, it probably would not matter much to her whether or not I went abroad; that the money consideration was the important factor.

To this, all she said was, 'You just go if you want to.'

In three more days I had to decide, but I found it most difficult to make up my mind. Was this a chance which ever afterwards I might regret not taking? Was this the escape from the bank I had prayed for for years? Would the amount I could send home from my salary in Ceylon make up for my being away?

It would mean the complete abandonment of my painting and my etching, but I would have to resign myself to that.

Would my grandmother be upset at my leaving?

I did hope that Annie would, on her own, talk over the subject with me; it would have made everything so much easier. I could not understand her determined silence in regard to a matter so vital to both of us.

I was no nearer a decision when the last day arrived. It happened that I was idly fingering an old silver coin found in the Foveran churchyard. Suddenly, I had the idea that I would let Fate decide for me. I would toss the coin three times, no, seven times, and abide by what the toss decided. On one side of the coin was a thistle device and if it fell showing the thistle it would indicate I must stay on.

Five times the thistle was uppermost, twice underneath. I was relieved to come to a decision even though I arrived at it by subterfuge.

After 'relieving' at Insch and Alford in the summer of 1904, I was sent in September to the recently opened Edinburgh branch. The office was short-staffed and for ten successive weekdays we worked till midnight, although not with the grim intensity I had been accustomed to. Also there was a camaraderie amongst the staff which did not exist in the Aberdeen offices.

The bank had appointed as the first manager of its Edinburgh office J. Milne Henderson—a chartered accountant of repute, with considerable influence in the capital. Within five minutes of my entering the office I was put in charge of the ledgers. Late on the evening of my second day, a Saturday, I was posting cheques into one of my ledgers when the manager, whom I now saw for the first time, quietly approached, mounted my low platform, stood alongside me, and began idly thumbing through a pile of paid-in slips on my desk. I was very busy, working against the midnight deadline of the Sabbath, but managed to steal an occasional glance at him.

He was, I saw, the antithesis of an Aberdeen banker, being thin, swarthy, with black moustache and short black beard, and grave but alert and penetrating black eyes. He wore an elegant waisted frock coat and moved with a suave grace. A Spanish grandee might look like that, I naively imagined.

Although he seemed engrossed in the paid-in slips I noticed that he was coming closer to me and I began to feel as though I were being stalked. Still turning them over, without looking at me, he said in very low tones,

'What church do you attend, Mr McBey?'

'None, sir.'

'What?'

'I attend no church, sir, I distrust all churches.'

'I am deeply shocked. Have you never attended church services?'

'Yes, sir, when a boy I had to attend the Established Church service every Sunday.'

'Did you not feel benefited?'

'Honestly, sir, I cannot say I did.'

'May I ask why?'

'Because I came to realise that church attendance was a mere formality on the part of the various congregations and besides, the sermons were vague and ambiguous.'

'Do you believe in prayer?'

'Yes, sir, but I have never felt the necessity for an intermediary.'

From his case he took a card, wrote on it with a gold pencil, handed it to me and said, 'This will give you the right to occupy my pew at my church tomorrow evening. I cannot attend. I want to know what you think of the sermon. The Revd. Mr T . . . , a famous preacher, is to occupy the pulpit.'

I thanked him and promised to attend. My fellow clerks, I could see, were most curious to know what our conversation had been about, and betrayed unmistakable suspicion. It occurred to me that they might regard me as a spy from Head Office, so I enlightened them slightly and learned that the manager was a deeply religious man and a pillar of his church.

On the Monday morning he beckoned me to his private room.

'Take this chair, Mr McBey.'

Never hitherto had I sat in the presence of a manager, an inspector or other high official; I felt myself an intruder.

'Now, Mr McBey, did you attend the service yesterday evening?'

'Yes, sir.'

'What did you think of the sermon? Were you impressed?' As I hesitated, he continued, 'I want you to be quite frank.'

'Well, sir, I was not impressed except by the preacher's command of language. He chose his text from the words of St Paul, in his first epistle to the Corinthians, "And now abideth faith, hope and charity, these three; but the greatest of these is charity". Although no one in the congregation would have disputed the point, he reiterated the statement and elaborated on the theme for three quarters of an hour and then related it closely to the collection which was to be taken at the close of his discourse. You asked me to be frank, sir.'

A faint wry smile formed itself. He reached out for a piece of paper, wrote on it, then, 'I have noted your criticism, Mr McBey, and I shall bring it to the notice of the Revd. Mr T . . .' He leant back and asked me with ingratiating blandness, 'Suppose, now, you were to suggest a text?'

'Well, sir, I should like to listen to a sermon based on Christ's words when he was nailed to the cross, "My God, My God, why hast Thou forsaken me".'

He regarded me sombrely for what seemed a long time then dismissed me with the words, 'I shall bring your suggested text to the notice of my friend. Meantime, as I have delayed you, you will no doubt be anxious to get on with your work.'

Frequently during my sojourn in Edinburgh he asked me to go to the services in different churches and report on them, but my suggested text was never again referred to. He regarded me, I felt, as an incorrigible heretic, but gradually between him, the manager, and me, a humble clerk, there came to exist an undertone of understanding.

When, later, the time came for the salaries to be reviewed by Head Office, he, unasked, went out of his way to commend me highly, but his suggestion was not acted upon; I belonged to Head Office, and was only lent to the Edinburgh office.

It happened that the accountant was the one under whom I had served four years of my apprenticeship in Aberdeen. I liked the life in Edinburgh but he did not, and wanted me to share his lodgings with him, this being the first time he had lived away from his home. I did so for several weeks, but when the urge to etch got me I wanted more privacy than was possible where we were.

I advertised in the *Evening News* and got over seventy replies. The whole staff turned themselves into experts and sifted these down to the nine most promising. Five of my fellow clerks then insisted on coming round these nine addresses with me, trooping noisily up interminable stairs and cross-examining potential landladies, asking them the most disconcerting questions.

Finally they decided on a room high up in one of the twin towers of a church at 44 Queen Street. It had a small window which looked right over part of Edinburgh, Leith, and right across the Forth to the hills of Fife. In my spare time I began etching Edinburgh subjects. I had not to search far in that most fascinating city.

There was a piece of carpet on the floor of my room. It was old and slightly tattered, but my landlady seemed to value it and began to get herself and me worried lest I might spill acid on it. So, instead of nitric acid I used perchloride of iron to bite my plates. I spoilt many of them owing to a deposit forming in the lines as I did not know then that I ought to have put my plates in the bath face downwards when using perchloride of iron.

After I had been four months in Edinburgh a parcel came for me with Aberdeen postmarks. It contained a black leather dressing case fitted with hair brushes, a cloth brush and toilet requisites, and had a slip of paper inside

on which was written in a strange handwriting the words
'from Annie'.

Nothing like this had ever happened before. I was certain
there must be some mistake. Why should Annie for no
apparent reason give me a present of a dressing case—one
bought at an expensive shop too? I waited days in the hope of
some explanation. I wanted so desperately to believe this act
was motivated by a sudden impulse of kindness on her part,
but I was so frightened of being let down and disappointed
that I forced myself to remain unaffected by it until I was
certain it was not all a mistake.

I found it most difficult to write her about the dressing
case. I knew that as she was now almost blind she would
have to get someone, possibly a neighbour, to read my letter
to her (my grandmother apparently knew nothing about the
present). I had to be careful lest I betrayed our unusual
relationship. And I would have felt humiliated and hurt if I
had mistakenly assumed the existence of an affection which
heretofore she had never shown.

I thanked her in such cautious terms that it would have
been easy for her to say there had been an error; the matter
was never again referred to.

In Edinburgh I had no access to a press, so I had to
wait until I was recalled to Aberdeen in March before
I could print my Edinburgh plates. Working over and
pulling proofs of them in the tense gloomy atmosphere
of Aberdeen brought vividly before me the difference in
my life in the two cities.

At the end of 1905 I, greatly daring, sent two etchings to
the Royal Scottish Academy, telling no one. One, 'Albert
Basin', was rejected, but the other, 'Old Torry'—a number
of herring fishing boats in the harbour of the Aberdeen
suburb—was hung.

I received the unexpected intimation with mixed feelings.
The elation I felt that my work was good enough to be
hung alongside that of real artists was balanced by an
uneasiness as to how the officials in the bank would regard
the unbankinglike employment of my spare time should they

come to know of it. I thought it advisable on the whole to keep dark my Edinburgh success.

A day later John Hutcheon—one of the inspectors—laid a folded *Aberdeen Free Press* in front of me, pointed to the tail of a paragraph, and said, 'Do you know anything about this?' I read the couple of lines at the end of the Royal Scottish Academy notice: 'Mr. James McBee, 42 Union Grove has an etching of "Old Torry".' My name was wrongly spelt.

'Yes, sir, that refers to me.'

'What is all this about? Do you make etchings?' He was not disapproving, only curious. I confessed how I had worked quietly for years, rising early every morning and working for an hour or two before I set out for the bank.

'Where did you learn to etch?'

'From a book which I borrowed from the Public Library.'

'How many etchings have you made?'

'About twenty-five.'

'I want to see them. Bring them down one day and I'll show them to the Directors of the Bank.'

Although not popular with most of the clerks, he had a bigness, poise, and an independence outstanding in that office where timid standards ruled. Nevertheless his sympathetic attitude was unexpected and gave me a great sense of relief, even a mild elation. No longer was it advisable that I work in secret. My etching being exhibited in the R.S.A. was an armour against the sarcasm I feared might come from my fellow clerks.

When, subsequently, I brought him about twenty-five of my Aberdeen, Portsoy, and Edinburgh etchings, he took them to the Directors' Room. When returning them to me he said the Directors admired them very much, adding that he had hoped some of them, who were wealthy and considered themselves collectors and patrons of art, might have purchased several but that unfortunately no one had done so.

I now felt bold enough to send two etchings to the Royal Glasgow Institute exhibition. Both were hung.

A week after the exhibition opened a letter came from someone offering me £2. 2s. 0d. for my two etchings. I had priced them at £1. 11s. 6d. each but I at once wrote accepting the offer, happy to know that someone was willing to buy my work. Although the amount was small, it was my first sale and Annie was impressed to the extent that she remarked, 'There must be something in these etchings you make, before anyone wants to spend money on them.'

I had always felt very cramped in our little prim parlour which was the only place I could use as a workshop. I hated having to put my gear and tools out of sight every day after use, but this concession I had been only too glad to make in return for the use of the room.

Parallel to Union Street ran a winding lane on to which opened the back entrances and stables of the big houses. Over one of these stables, 22 Justice Hill Lane, was a loft with a 'to let' notice nailed to it. The side which faced the street was nearly all window made up of irregular-sized panes of obscured glass. Every time I passed along the lane I paused and imagined what a wonderful studio the place would make.

Day by day I accumulated courage and finally bearded the owner—a woman, apparently wealthy, who lived in the big house in Union Street corresponding to the stable. She told me the rent she wanted was £10 a year and gave me the key along with that of the stable underneath through which one had to pass to get to the yard where was a wooden stair leading to the loft. The stable she told me was let to an officer of the Gordon Highlanders who stabled his 'horseless carriage' in it.

The loft I found was large, about 40 feet square, dilapidated, but apparently watertight. From the low ceiling hung a gas bracket with a single jet.

When I returned the keys I offered the landlady £8 for a year's rent, pointing out that as the fireplace had been bricked up there was no means of heating the place. Reluctantly she agreed to give me a year's lease at that figure. I made one condition: that as I was paying rent in advance she would not mention my name or associate me in any way to anyone else in connection with the renting of her loft.

In the dark of the evenings I moved in a tripod easel, my box of paints, three or four canvasses, a small table, my etching press, and a wooden packing case in which I had made shelves. These articles made an incongruous little group in the large empty space of the loft. I was quite proud of this, my first studio, and I luxuriated in a heavenly sensation of privacy.

In those autumn evenings I laboured at two oil paintings from elaborate pencil sketches I had made in the summer. One was of a field of white daisies with, in the middle distance, two girls each with an armful of them; the other of two boys on the steep wild-rose-covered bank of a brook in which they were fishing.

To account for my absence from home whilst working in my loft I had to pretend I was studying in the reference department of the library. As I was careful to be home by 9 p.m. every night no suspicions were aroused.

As the autumn daylight shortened to the winter I had to work wholly by the light of my single gas jet. It was an eerie sensation to stand and paint in a small patch of light which did not reach any wall of the loft, amid a silence which magnified the slightest sound I made.

As winter approached the cold became intense, and even wearing an overcoat and mittens I could work for only an hour or two at a time.

Underneath me was stabled the horseless carriage of the Gordon Highlanders officer. It was a formidable red-painted, dangerous-looking contraption with four elaborate oil lamps and abundant solid polished brass fittings. It exuded a peculiar pungent odour which charged the whole atmosphere of its stable through which I had to pass every time I entered or left my loft. The owner of the premises had impressed on me that, as the machine was liable to catch fire, and probably explode, very easily, I must never use a naked light in the stable. Knowing nothing about the new horseless carriages, I treated her injunction with respect and night after night, in total darkness, I felt my way around the pro-tuberances of the smelly vehicle to the doors of the stable.

One night—the 11th of December 1906—I worked later than usual. From pencil sketches I was painting in a small figure of an old woman gathering driftwood on the beach at Catterline. It gave me a lot of trouble and I had to wipe it out several times. I became so engrossed that I lost count of time and stopped only when my hands became too cold to hold the brush. It was nearly 9.30 p.m. when I reached home. Both my grandmother and Annie had gone to bed.

At 2.30 a.m. I was awakened by my grandmother shaking my shoulder. In the light of the candle which she carried her face had a perplexed look.

'Annie is not in her bed.'

Knowing that Annie often spent night hours sitting muffled up in the parlour I replied,

'She is probably in the parlour.'

'No, I have looked there.'

'Then where could she be? She could not have gone out alone. We must just search everywhere we can think of.'

I opened the door to the stairs and listened. All was quiet. There was only one other place I could think of—a very unlikely one.

'She may have gone to the cellar for some reason and tripped over something. I'll go down and look.'

My grandmother replied, 'I think I'll come with you.'

'All right, but it's bitterly cold.'

Together we went down slowly and softly and apprehensively, I holding the candlestick. We reached the basement and turned into the open space in front of the cellar doors.

There, in the dim light cast by my candle, stood Annie fully clothed. Behind me my grandmother called gently, 'Why are you down here in the cold?' Suddenly the hairs of my body stood up. I saw that Annie's feet were not touching the ground.

I turned in front of my grandmother.

'Come back upstairs. I must get my knife.'

She looked at me for a moment perplexed before her eyes dilated. She turned without a word. I helped her

James McBey's grandmother, Mary Gillespie. *Painting* (1901)

James McBey's mother, Anne Gillespie.

James McBey, aged three.

Boys fishing. *Etching* (1902)

The Blacksmith's Shop. *Etching* (1903)

Portsoy Harbour. *Etching* (1903)

Enkhuisen Harbour. *Etching* (1910)

The Mill, Zaandijk. *Etching* (1910)

Hoorn Cheesemarket. *Etching* (1910)　　　A Volendam Girl. *Etching* (1910)

Omval. *Etching* (1910)

above left: The Cowgate, Edinburgh.
Etching (1904-5)

above right: Inverleith.
Etching (1904-5)

left: Warriston Close.
Etching (1905)

Herring Fleet, Aberdeen.
Etching (1908)

left: Waiting for the Boats, Portlethen.
Etching (1909)

The Dean Bridge, Edinburgh. *Etching* (1904).

upstairs, made her sit down, forbad her to move, and got my pocket knife.

Quickly I tiptoed back to the basement and set my candle-stick on the floor. It took all my courage to approach the silent figure turning so slightly. I reached up and cut the two cords above her head. She fell heavily at my feet. With difficulty I undid the noose almost embedded in her neck, my fingers fumbled so. Her head and hands were quite cold.

I hurried upstairs making no noise as I was barefooted. My grandmother was exactly as I had left her. I lit a lamp. I told her I was going to fetch a doctor, to put on warm clothes and not to leave the room or make any noise. She appeared dazed but nodded understanding. I was fearful that one of the other tenants sleeping all round us would get to know anything of this night's happenings.

Quietly I got my cycle downstairs. I knew no doctor, but I cycled towards Bon-accord Square on the railing of which were many doctors' brass plates. I rang the bell of the first one—a Dr Wyness. After what seemed an interminable wait he opened the door, and took me into his waiting-room.

'What can I do for you?'

'My mother (it was with a conscious effort I used those two words) has hanged herself at 42 Union Grove. Will you come with me.'

'If she has hanged herself, I can do nothing. You must go to the police.'

He showed me out, and I mounted my cycle and sped down silent Union Street.

A black cat darting across the street ran right underneath my forewheel, throwing me off. Fortunately my cycle was not twisted. The police station was, to my intense relief, partially open.

I had never been inside a police station. I knew not what to expect and certainly did not anticipate sympathy. Now, in front of a uniformed official at a desk, I found myself very calm. Guardedly I said, 'I have to report a suicide.' He looked searchingly at me for a few seconds then without a word went to another room and returned accompanied by another officer.

'This is Inspector Wilson. He will take charge of the case. Please sit down and answer his questions.' The inspector wrote down my replies on a sheet of paper which they handed me to sign. The officer then said, 'You have a cycle outside. The inspector will go with you.'

Side by side, without a word being spoken, the inspector and I cycled up to Union Grove.

'Is the body still in the basement?'

'Yes, I'll show you where. Would you come as quietly as possible?'

He followed close behind me to the basement, lighting the way with his bulls-eye lantern.

He flashed his light all around and on Annie's body. He scrutinised closely the deep groove around her neck, then asked. 'Where is the rope?' An end of rope was projecting from beneath her dress. This I handed to him. He examined it closely. Instantly he was all suspicion, and drew himself up.

'This rope is not cut.'

'Then there must be another piece somewhere.'

He turned his lantern and there behind him lay the piece which had formed the noose. This and the other cut piece which still hung from the beam of the low ceiling he examined very closely.

'I'll take those pieces of rope. Do any of your neighbours know what has happened?'

'No one, so far.'

'All right. You help me and we'll carry the body upstairs.'

Between us we carried Annie to where my grandmother was seated, waiting, and laid her body gently on the floor of the parlour. He asked my grandmother the same questions as he had asked me at the police station. She replied with a calmness and a lucidity which must have impressed him. I asked him anxiously, 'Will all this be in the press?'

'I shall do my best to prevent it. There is no public inquest but you will have to be examined by the Procurator

Fiscal. I will hide the charge book for a few days and at the headquarters we'll say to the reporters it has been mislaid. Once several days pass it will be stale news and they will not print anything about it. Take your grandmother back to the kitchen. I'll put things as straight as I can before it is too late.'

No words that I knew could have expressed the gratitude I felt towards Inspector Wilson.

After he had gone I remembered I had left my cycle outside in the street. When I went to bring it upstairs a policeman standing beside it in the darkness asked me in low tones, 'Have you seen Inspector Wilson?'

'Yes, he left an hour ago.'

'Are you James McBey?'

'Yes.'

'You were at the Police Station and gave your age as 22. They sent me up to get your correct age.'

'That *is* my correct age.'

'All right, only they were sure there had been a mistake. They wondered if you meant 32.'

'I made no mistake. My age is 22.'

He mounted his cycle and rode off.

With infinite caution I began the awkward job of getting my cycle up the dark stairway without making any noise. When halfway up I decided to take it down to the cellar space as, should any of the tenants have heard anything, my taking my cycle downstairs might be thought to account for the unusual sounds.

Returning upstairs I found my grandmother had lit the kitchen fire and was preparing to cook a pot of porridge. She had complete control of herself. In silence the two of us began our meal—the first we had ever had alone.

I asked her, 'Did Annie say anything last night?'

'Not a word. We went to bed as usual about 9 o'clock.'

'Did she act in an unusual manner?'

'Not that I noticed.'

'Where could she have got the rope? She must have had it

hidden somewhere. It looks as if she must have determined on this some time ago.'

'That is what I was thinking.'

We searched our memories and analysed every chance remark we could recall having been made by Annie for weeks past but could remember nothing which might have indicated to us her secret resolve.

Once more I went down to the basement and made a thorough search, lest some scrap of evidence of the tragedy might have been overlooked.

I found nothing.

When dawn came, bringing with it the accustomed activities of our neighbours, it was with incredible relief that we came to realise that no one was apparently aware of the nightmare we had passed through. Like two conspirators, my grandmother and I discussed the possibility that they might never even know, although the chances seemed very very slim. We agreed to say Annie died of heart failure.

I telephoned the accountant at the bank, to whose department I had been transferred, hoping he would be too busy to take more interest than to fill my place temporarily.

When the undertakers came they looked curiously at the black-clothed figure lying on the parlour floor. The elder of the two men bent down suspiciously and looked closely at the neck. Suddenly he stood upright and said to me, 'We cannot touch this.'

'The police know all about it.'

'Were they here?'

'Yes, Inspector Wilson made an examination. He was satisfied it was suicide.'

'I ought to communicate with them, but I'll take your word for it.'

'No one knows of this but the police and my grandmother. Could you in some way conceal the mark on the neck?'

He became sympathetic. 'It will not be easy, but you can trust me to do my best.'

In an hour or two it would be necessary for me to go to the offices of the local press and insert the notice of Annie's death. I was dubious about leaving my grandmother to handle the situation if the neighbours learned about Annie's death in my absence, so I myself told those with whom we were on more friendly terms. They were very sympathetic and obviously suspected nothing.

My grandmother did not apparently mind being left alone, but I took the precaution of locking the door of the parlour, giving her the key and impressing on her to allow no one into the room except the undertakers. She calmly said I could rely on her, that my advice was quite unnecessary.

Although we had lived together all my life I began to see her in a new light. Her energy in doing all the cooking and general housework I had been accustomed to take for granted as the years passed, not heeding the fact that, although her hair was only just beginning to run from mouse-colour to grey, she had already reached the age of 87. Now I realised how tough and unimpaired she actually was and that she could be trusted to hold her own in the situation which Fate had thrust upon us.

The undertakers returned before nightfall. Before he left, the elder of the two men asked me to come to the parlour and see what they had done.

Lying in her coffin Annie looked strangely serene. The fretful lines had all gone from her forehead and the now relaxed lips took all trace of grimness from her mouth. She appeared to be dreaming happily and looked much younger than when alive.

I gazed so long at the unexpected transformation that the undertakers had to draw my attention to the frill on the neck-band of the shroud, which had been made purposely wide. He cautioned me, 'You will have to be careful no one touches that frill. It hides the mark on the neck, but only just.'

Next day it was unlikely that any neighbours or acquaintances would come to pay their respects till the afternoon. I wanted to be alone for an hour or two, so in the forenoon I walked to the almost deserted embankment by the river Dee.

It was a still, frosty morning. A grey haze rising high above the houses lay on the city. Through its upper edge the sun, a ball of red gold, tried to penetrate. All sounds seemed muted. The sight of everyone quietly going about their business as though nothing had happened awoke in me a sense of seclusion, even of security.

Now, alone by the river bank, I could review in my mind the change in my circumstances. I felt I ought to be ashamed of a lurking buoyancy which, in spite of my every effort to suppress it, kept thrusting itself amongst my thoughts.

I wondered why Annie had gone without a single word or gesture of farewell. What feelings did she in her heart bear towards me? Did she attribute my coming into existence as the source of all her trouble, worry, and eventual blindness? Was her final act long premeditated?

I searched my memory for anything I might have said or done which could have precipitated the sombre thoughts she must have harboured during her years of night, but I could recall nothing except perhaps my too cautious thanks for the dressing case she had sent me two years previously.

My thoughts took a bitter turn. Perhaps the determined isolation in which she took refuge was because of a conviction she may have formed that she was an outcast—a social leper. Had she, back in Newburgh days, had to suffer slights that, as darkness overcame her, became in her mind more and more of an obsession which at the last became no longer endurable? Did she feel that for the last half of her life everyone had been against her and did she, in a flash of omniscience, feel that she had handed on a taint and that every man's hand would be against mine?

These and similar speculations kept revolving in my head as I walked slowly back. Even the word 'home' had a new connotation. No longer did it signify merely a lair or a refuge. No longer need the affection between my grandmother and myself have to be furtive nor our loyalty to each other concealed.

No one called that day.

Next day several of the neighbours and a few Newburgh

friends called. Each one, conforming to custom, laid a hand on the cold forehead for a brief second. All the time, my heart thumping, I was standing close beside the body, watchful that no hand or sleeve would disturb the frill around the neck and disclose what lay beneath.

My grandmother and I had conspired between us that not more than two persons should be in the parlour at one time, as I feared that if by ill chance they discovered anything I might have to swear them to secrecy.

I remembered having read that suicides were denied burial in consecrated ground by some of the religious sects; I had forgotten which. Perhaps the Church of Scotland subscribed to this curious proscription but I did not dare enquire. I felt it would be a last act of loyalty to Annie if I could ensure that she were not treated as a pariah in death, that she would have her rightful place with her contemporaries amongst the crowded headstones under the trees in the quiet damp churchyard of Foveran.

On the forenoon of the funeral I went alone to the parlour. As I gazed on her face for the last time I fell to wondering why she had never shown any sign of affection. To the best of my recollection she had never kissed me. Yet it was possible that by leaving as she did she felt she would be making life less difficult for me.

The hearse, followed by one carriage in which were her two brothers and myself, slowly wound its way through the twelve miles of deep mud and cold drizzle, taking three hours to make the journey. At the graveside the service was short. The rain dripping from the bare overhanging branches of the trees alone disturbed the melancholy silence of the churchyard of Foveran, where Annie now lay safe in consecrated soil.

V

At this time I was in charge of the 'clearing desk' at the bank. One of my duties was to go every afternoon to the manager in his room and show him my book wherein were the totals of the cheques cleared by the various banks that day.

He was a big stout man with a large bald head, features resembling Bismarck and an abrupt manner, never wasting a word. Invariably, day after day, he glanced at the amounts in my list and gave a grunt of acknowledgement.

I had been absent for three days. On the first day I resumed work after the funeral no one had remarked on my absence, or the reason for it, until, when I was showing the manager my totals, he said, to my astonishment, 'You have been ill?'

'No sir, my mother died.'

'What did she die of?'

His question was so unexpected I failed to prevaricate.

'She committed suicide.'

'What?'

'She hanged herself.'

His solemn pale bulbous eyes glanced up at me from their red rims for a second, then without a word he resumed his writing of a letter. (More than twenty years afterwards, long after he had retired from the bank, several of his friends were, in his presence, commenting on the extraordinary luck which Providence had seen fit to bestow on me. His terse contribution to the discussion—'I'm sorry for that man'—completely mystified the group. This was told me later by one who was present, possibly on the chance I might elucidate the remark.)

On my way home that first day I saw from a distance a dense group of people clustering in front of the *Free Press* office, each individual striving to read the news bill apparently newly hung out in front of the window. Alarm seized me. It could only mean that the press had found out and published that which I prayed might remain secret.

Cautiously, in utter dread of what I might see, I attached myself to the edge of the group waiting my chance to get a glimpse of what I feared. I started violently when a hand strongly gripped my arm, and turned to face Inspector Wilson. In a low voice, without preamble, he said in my ear, 'Don't worry; they've discovered nothing. I think you're safe now.'

My relief was so great that my knees almost gave way.

Annie, I knew, used to have a few personal trinkets in a small wooden box she kept locked. Several days after the funeral I found a key which opened it. The contents consisted of a string of blackish sweet-smelling beads, like sheep droppings, that my grandmother recalled my wearing when a baby, a small gold watch that had belonged to Jane, Annie's silver watch, and a silver locket and its chain. Inside the locket was a photo of Annie as a girl and behind the glass facing it, a small folded scrap of newsprint.

Gently flattening it out, not knowing what to expect, I found, trimly torn from a newspaper, a poem entitled

'The Suicide'
No one will weep
or sigh that I had gone.
One half the uncaring world will sleep,
the other struggle on.

When I read it out to my grandmother we looked at one another in amazement. Neither of us knew that this scrap of newsprint existed. It seemed to have been in the locket for a very long time. We compared memories as to how many years had passed since Annie had been able to read. Fifteen at least. Where had she seen it and how long ago was it since she had hidden it in her locket? What was in her mind when she put it there? And did she intend it to be discovered there or had she herself forgotten all about it? We knew it was impossible that anyone else could have read it to her. The more we discussed it the more mysterious it became.

Annie had been buried less than a fortnight when George—the younger of her two brothers—sent me a letter couched in an aggressive tone intimating that it was high time I produced Annie's will. I replied informing him that Annie's wealth was just under £150; that it would have been considerably less had I not, for the seven years I had been earning, contributed the bulk of my salary towards our joint support, and that she had left no will as the money was in our joint names payable to either or survivor.

Two months later he again wrote me saying that he was getting deeper and deeper into debt and asking me to lend him £150. I had always had a liking for George and he was my grandmother's favourite son. He was a skilful craftsman but had little resistance when the rounds of whiskies began at the pubs. I was minded to lend him the £150 but had to think out a way whereby there was a chance I would be repaid at some future date, as that was all the money I possessed.

I read his letter to my grandmother, who, I could see, had a lurking sympathy with him in his difficulties. I said to her I would be willing to lend him the money if she would agree to make a will ensuring that George's debt be repaid me from the share of her estate which would fall to him. She thought well of my scheme. As Willie, the eldest son, was indirectly concerned, I felt he ought to be cognisant of what was afoot. My grandmother agreed and I went purposely to tell him.

A thin bitter smile shaped itself round Willie's mouth as he listened to me. When he had heard the full proposal he became strangely enraged.

'Now I'll tell you something. A week ago George came to see me here. He sat on that very chair you are on now and proposed to me that I join him in getting a lawyer to try and take from you all the money which belonged to Annie. I told him I didn't want to have anything to do with it. Why he came to me was because somebody would have to pay the lawyer and that would be me.'

'Willie, I can hardly believe that of George.'

'Well you please yourself, but it's the God's truth. All George wants is to get his hands on your money, and then you can whistle for it.'

I was loth to disclose George's treachery to my grand-mother; she should keep her illusions. I told her Willie did not think well of her making a will because of the expense and possible complications. She seemed a trifle disappointed at first, then said, 'Ah well, I suppose he'll manage. I never did care for his wife.'

To George's request for a loan I replied that I had myself need of the money and could not spare it. I never again heard from him, nor did I ever see him.

My nerves had been shaken. I found that I could no longer work in my loft after darkness came down. I tried, but at the slightest sound I started and looked fearfully around me, dreading I might see a dark figure suspended in the gloom.

As the spring evenings lengthened their light I gradually got control of myself but I never again felt at ease in that silent building.

I painted from sketches a landscape of Benachie which I sent at the close of the year to the 12th Exhibition of the Aberdeen Artists Society. Although it was skied high above a doorway, I was very pleased that at last one painting of mine had been exhibited on the same footing as those of genuine artists.

My year's lease of the loft expired in the autumn. I did not renew it; instead I rented a room up three flights of stairs in an office building at 220 Union Street. Here, from all round me came the faint friendly sounds of civilisation which at the same time gave me a sense of comfort.

It was now that Robert Watt, the manager of the Commercial Road branch of the bank, whose son had worked alongside me in the George Street office, took a bold step. He commissioned me to paint his portrait for what was a noble sum to me—£15—and gave me a free hand as regards the execution.

He was a stout man of a kindly, hearty nature. He had little enough reason to assume that I could paint a portrait which he would dare hang on his wall, but he took the risk; his motive may have been a purely generous one.

I nailed together a platform; he brought a chair from his office and the sittings commenced.

Into the portrait I put all I knew about painting. When finished, it was really rather like him. It certainly could not be mistaken for anyone else, was the conclusion his family came to. They happened to bring in the family fox terrier on one occasion they came to see the finished work. The little dog stood tense in front of it, the hair on his back rose and he emitted plaintive yelps. I knew little of the ways of dogs, and consequently I was thankful of the family's assurance that here was proof conclusive that the likeness must be a good one.

This portrait I sent to the Aberdeen Artists Society Exhibition in November 1908 along with three etchings—Portsoy Harbour, Old Torry, and Albert Basin, each of which I priced at £2. 2s. 0d. Although the portrait was placed hard in the corner of two walls, I was pleased that all four works were accepted and hung. And the *Free Press* in its review of the show actually mentioned me:

'Mr. James McBey has several noteworthy exhibits, two being "Old Torry" and "Albert Basin, Aberdeen". The work is clear but some may perhaps consider suffers a little from overcrowding and fullness of detail.'

The faint praise kept disturbing me. Like my grandmother, I had a simple-minded awe of the printed word and for me to question this oracular dictum would have been rank sacrilege.

Naively I hoped that someone might make an offer for my etchings or even ask my fee for painting a portrait, and I imagined myself having the courage to ask fifteen or even twenty pounds. The exhibition closed without either an offer or an enquiry coming my way.

At the bank the clerk in charge of the 'stationery desk' had fallen ill from overwork. His predecessor had met the same fate. I was transferred to the desk, which was a miniature department in itself, and I found I was to become a sort of buying agent for the Bank. From a score of bookbinders, printers and stationers in Aberdeen, all good clients of the Bank, it was my job to purchase at the very lowest possible price all the ledgers, books, printed material and paper that the Bank and its 152 branches throughout Scotland required, amounting to almost £20,000 a year. Also, I had to distribute to each branch its supplies, keep a meticulous record of this and at the same time make sure it got no more than its necessary quota. Any unusual demand from a branch had to be investigated; all this to guard against possible waste.

The debts I incurred to the various firms were paid monthly after I had first submitted the accounts to the manager and the secretary, John Innes, who eight years previously had been the inspector who had examined me for entrance to the Bank. He held a private inquisition on the accounts I showed him each month, comparing my handling unfavourably with that of my predecessors, and always seemed chagrined that he could discover no discrepancy or overpayment. I knew he would make the most of it should he detect an error, so I became wary and alive to the danger in his crafty and softly-asked questions.

The manager's attitude was very different. He trusted me to keep the prices as low as possible and prevent waste, and regarded me as a diplomatic buffer between him and the different firms, each of which was jealous of the others and kept trying to get more than its fair share of the Bank's business.

The work was far too much for one person. I learned that at the annual balance in September my predecessors had had to work till midnight for three weeks or a month tracking down some elusive, piddling error. When I tried a balance I came to within £5, but after working late for three nights the hopelessness of searching through the many thousands of entries made throughout the past twelve months, many of them by my predecessor, appalled me.

What gave me concern, besides, was that I imagined I had become more shortsighted in the past year or two, due perhaps to eye strain, and had recently taken to wearing glasses constantly in an effort to relieve it. I knew the specialists at the Infirmary had failed to prevent my mother becoming blind and deep in my mind I dreaded the possibility that I might have inherited some incurable defect.

Because of this and because I did not relish the prospect of my becoming the third victim of the stationery desk I decided to 'cook the books', say nothing about it, and trust to my getting away with it. I could not see that it would matter to anyone as my books formed an integral system, and no cash transactions were involved.

Somewhat unwisely, as it turned out, I made them balance exactly, to a penny.

The accountant's department, to which I was attached, was entirely separate from the inspection department; between the two existed a latent jealousy.

I made out my balance sheet—a model of accuracy— and took it to the inspector's room to have it signed by an inspector.

He greeted me affably, dipped his pen in ink, glanced down my balance sheet and poised his pen to sign. Instead of signing he leant back in his chair.

'Your books balance exactly, Mr McBey?'

I saw the mistake I had made. My predecessors must have shown a discrepancy and thrown themselves on the mercy of the inspectors. Realising quickly that I had gone too far to do the same and that I must bluff it out, I replied, 'Yes, sir.'

'Weren't you surprised when they balanced to a penny?'

'I was both surprised and thankful, Mr McGregor.'

To the first inspector, seated across the room, he said, 'The stationery books balance to a penny this year, Mr Reid.'

Mr Reid: 'This is probably the first time in the Bank's history that this has happened. You must be pretty expert, Mr McBey.'

'Thank you, sir.'

Mr McGregor: 'I'll keep your balance sheet for a little, Mr McBey, and have a look at it at my leisure.'

The war was on.

Later in the day I went to the accountant, the head of my department.

'My books show an exact balance, Mr Stuart.'

'That's splendid.'

'Perhaps, but the inspectors do not believe it and have not signed the balance sheet.'

He looked quite alarmed.

'But they did balance, didn't they?'

'Almost, but I'll take the responsibility if an inspector finds anything.'

'I hope for your sake they will not.'

A few days later the inspector checked the quantities in my stock room with my books. As he went from shelf to shelf counting the bundles and the piles of ledgers an amusing relationship developed between us. When, towards the end of his arduous quest, he found everything correct he began to treat his task more and more as a joke. He was certain I had 'cooked' something somewhere and he knew that I knew he knew it. What nettled him was that the amount might happen to be a large one and moreover his professional skill as a sleuth was at stake.

When, a month later, the Bank's auditors came, the formidable Chartered Accountant and his staff closeted themselves with my records. After three days my books were brought back to me without comment.

When, at the time of the next annual balance, I took in my sheet showing, again, an exact balance, Mr McGregor signed it in silence, but the look he gave me as he handed it back was, I felt, one he would have bestowed on a rattlesnake should he ever have had to encounter one.

I grew to like the stationery desk. The work, although onerous, had relatively little responsibility attached to it and I was brought increasingly in contact with many varied types of men and their moods and foibles. Human nature fascinated me.

The Bank had amalgamated with the 'Town and County', a small bank. The directors, now seventeen in number, met on Wednesday in their palatial room upstairs. We ordinary mortals caught a glimpse of the Olympians as they entered or left the bank ignoring our existence.

One forenoon the manager, passing my desk, stopped.

'I want you to get seventeen folding blotter cases with a pocket in each, for the directors. Get the best you can find.'

'There are no such blotters on sale, but I can get them made specially.'

'All right, get them good.'

'I can get them of real Russian leather, but that will be expensive.'

He hesitated a moment, gulped, then deliberately fitted words into a sequence unknown within those walls:

'In this case expense does not matter.'

The cases were duly made of the smooth wine-coloured leather, that smelt so attractively of the birch bark tanning. I showed him one for his approval.

'Excellent, how much?'

'Thirty-seven and sixpence each.'

'H'm. Now I should like you to get each director's name stamped in gold on the outside of his case.'

'Yes, sir.'

When handing the bookbinder a list of the directors' names it occurred to me that if the letters were stamped on the leather binding, cases would become useless if for any reason changes occurred in the directorate. I instructed the binder to stamp the names in gold on oblongs of the same leather, tool in gold the edges of the oblongs, and paste them on the outside of the cases.

When finished accordingly, I took them to the manager's room. The secretary, Mr Innes, was also in the room. The manager was pleased with them, but the secretary, examining one closely, detected the oblongs in which the names were printed.

'What does this mean, Mr McBey? I suppose you have been sold flaws in the leather beneath these.'

'No, sir, these oblongs are intentional.'

'Why?'

'Because the cases are expensive, and none need now be wasted if there are changes amongst the directors, as the oblongs can be easily taken off.'

'What changes do you anticipate amongst our directors, Mr McBey?'

'Well, sir, they seem all fairly old men to me and the cases will outlast them.'

The manager gave an unprecedented chuckle and the secretary, taking his cue from that, said in his low vinegary voice, 'Your idea, Mr McBey, is a very economical one, but naturally we shall not disclose to the fairly old men who constitute our directorate why easily replaced pieces of leather are used on which to stamp their names on their blotters.'

Searching for a receptacle of some sort in which to keep my papers in my 'studio', I looked in occasionally at the weekly auction sales of furniture.

I could afford only a small sum, but luckily a bureau was knocked down to me for £1. 15s. 0d. It was an honest homely piece of craftmanship, made of solid oak, friendly to the eye. (Years later I learned it was Dutch and about 200 years old.) Now, I wanted a chair to go with it. I went to view the articles advertised for sale in a small auction room in Crown Street. The 'antique chair' which I thought might interest me was riddled with worm holes and useless for my purpose.

On a table near it I noticed what appeared to be a plaster half-head, life size, stained or painted dark brown, with the number '31' chalked on the forehead. Mildly curious, I tried to pick it up by its nose and found it unexpectedly heavy. It was bronze, not plaster. In the printed list of the articles to be auctioned the number 31 was a complete blank; apparently the auctioneer was at a loss to know how to classify or describe it. This was interesting, and I examined it more closely. It was not a piece of sculpture but a cast from a human face and, as the jaw and lips were relaxed, probably a death mask. The light was dim but it was possible to decipher, incised along one side of the v forming the throat, a name—F. ANTOMMARCHI. Somewhere I had seen that name, but where, though I stirred my memory deeply, I could not recall.

Early next morning—the day of the sale—it suddenly came to me. Antommarchi was the Corsican surgeon mentioned in Lord Rosebery's *Napoleon: The Last Phase*.

I adjusted my work in the bank so that I could for fifteen minutes or so attend the sale, resolved to bid up to £2 for the bronze, that amount being all I could afford. Unfortunately I was delayed and when I reached the auction room the sale was just over. I asked the clerk what No. 31 fetched.

'Number thirty-one; it was a bronze face, wasn't it? It brought six shillings and ninepence; Middleton, who has that little second-hand shop in Marischal Street, bought it.'

Middleton's little second-hand shop was within three minutes' walk of the bank and it was easy for me to take a frequent look at the clutter of dilapidated junk in the small window. If I showed interest in or eagerness to purchase the bronze he would, I feared, ask a figure beyond the £2 I could afford. Then, late on the afternoon of the third day, there it was resting serenely on a pile of stained trousers. Although the afternoon was cold, a thunderstorm with frequent flashes of lightning was growling overhead.

As I entered, one of three women seated round a big fire rose and asked what I wanted.

'Could I see that bronze head in your window?'
She climbed over a pile of blankets and umbrellas but when about to take hold of the bronze, she hesitated and said,

'Do you mind getting it yourself?'

'Not a bit, but why don't you just hand it to me?'

'I have my reasons.'
I climbed over the umbrellas, got the bronze, and regained the floor. She addressed me.

'Do you want to buy it?'

'Yes, if I can afford the price you ask for it.'

'My man told me not to sell it. That it was very valuable. What did you want it for?'

'I am an artist. I wanted it so that I could make drawings of it.'

'It would be good for that. Pity it's not for sale.' (Pointing to the incised name.) 'Is that the man who cut it out?'

'It is not cut out. It is cast off a corpse.'
At that word one of the two women seated at the fire who had so far taken no interest in the proceedings turned round and said, 'I told you that was taken off a dead body; I would na' have it in the place.'

As I held it with the lightning flashes glinting on one side of the face and the red firelight glowing on the other, it did look a formidable object. Disappointed, I said, 'Well, if you do decide to sell it let me know, I'll give you my name.'

As I turned to leave the first woman said, 'Here, take the damned thing with you; I hate it; give me the six and nine-pence my man paid for it at Reid's sale.'

'What, are you frightened of it?'

'Yes, my boy put a bonnet on it and stuck it up at the foot of my bed and scared me. I'll be glad to see the last of it.'

Six weeks later the dealer Middleton accosted me and asked, 'Are you the man who bought a bronze head from my wife?'

'Yes.'

'Have you found out whose head it was?'

'I have hung it in the Northern Arts Club to see if any of the members can tell. Why do you ask?'

'Because two men came a fortnight ago to my shop asking about it. We lost your name. They appeared very disappointed at losing it. They didn't leave their names.'

Years afterwards I learned it was one of the original death-masks of Napoleon, cast by Dr Antommarchi from the front half of the gypsum mould made of the dead emperor at St Helena by Dr Burton—the mould which was stolen by Madame Bertrand and lent by her to Antommarchi.

Part of my duty in the bank was to act as sixth teller to relieve the pressure of customers, usually from 2.30 to 3.30 every day and all day on Saturdays.

Working at a broad open counter in full view of the customers on the public's side, I noticed that strangers used to regard my hands with, to me, an interest which became uncomfortable and I grew sensitive about the enlarged raw joints on the second fingers of each hand—the legacy from my schooldays. Try as I would, I could not resist automatically snipping off the roughnesses with my teeth.

Some drastic cure for this habit had to be tried.

I bent my fingers, and inverted them both for a half inch or so into the nitric acid in the etching bath, holding them until the mordant had bitten well in. The flesh became a bright yellow, then a dull yellow, then formed itself into hard bosses which after three weeks detached themselves in the form of two hollow caps, leaving underneath clean soft flesh. The three weeks during which the bitter taste of the nitric-impregnated skin had prevented me from biting them, had cured me completely.

The Scottish banks accumulated gold in the form of sovereigns and half sovereigns, due, perhaps, to the mysterious workings of some economic law or racial characteristic.

It was the Bank's practice to send its surplus gold twice a year to its correspondent bank in London—the Union of London and Smiths Bank. The bullion was in sealed canvas bags containing £1,000 each and ten of those bags were packed together in a strong wooden case with rope handles—this also with impressive seals on the outside. The consignment was then put on the night train to London and conveyed during its thirteen-hour journey by an inspector and one of the younger clerks.

It was generally believed in the office that the inspector was armed with a revolver, although none of us was certain on this point.

Each of us small fry hoped one day to be chosen to accompany an inspector on the trip to London which was regarded in the office as in the nature of a joy-ride. It started invariably on a Monday evening and the lucky participant had a holiday of six clear days as he was not expected to be at work till the following Monday morning. Besides, he was given £3 for his week's expenses.

I entertained no hope for myself considering the suspicion I had unquestionably aroused in the minds of the inspectors by my faultless balance sheets.

Every afternoon as the closing hour of 3 p.m. drew near the customers crowded in front of the long curving mahogany counter. One Monday afternoon the manager, passing my box, stopped and said in his abrupt way: 'You'll have to go to London with the gold tonight. Better stop now and get ready.' He passed on without another word; I thought my ears had played a trick on me.

Customers were two deep in front of us six tellers. I leant towards the teller next to me and asked him, 'Did you hear what I think I heard the manager say?'

'He said you had to stop and go to London with the gold. I suppose now I'll have to take your customers.'

Quickly, I balanced my cash and sped home. I packed a bag, told my grandmother I would have to be away for nearly a week, arranged with a neighbour to see her as often as possible, and hurried back to the bank.

On my way I purchased at a bookseller's a guide to London with plans of the streets.

As I drew near the office I overtook a shy young clerk who was in the Securities Department. Like me he carried a small bag.

'Hello, Willox, you're going on a journey?'

'I'm going to London with the gold.'

'What's that? The manager told me I was going.'

'I know you are.'

'Are three of us going?'

'No, but all the inspectors are away and you're to be in charge.'

One of the porters admitted us to the now closed bank. On the mosaic floor in front of the counter were twelve wooden boxes with large red seals, guarded by the two porters and the head of the Securities Department from whom I asked, 'What are my instructions? I was not told I was to be in charge of this consignment.'

'You will have to be very, very careful. This is a special consignment, the biggest we have ever sent. Each of those boxes contains £10,000. All the railway can give us at such short notice is an ordinary first-class compartment. I think we shall be able to fit in the boxes with you two fellows as well, but you mustn't both sleep at the same time.'

'I see, but shouldn't I have a revolver?'

'Do you know how to use a revolver?'

'No, I have never even had one in my hands.'

'Then you are probably safer without one. And, if there should be an accident, try to communicate with the Bank, but on no account must you both lose sight of the boxes.'

'All right, now what happens when we reach London?'

'Have you ever been to London?'

'Heavens, no, I have never been outside Scotland.'

'Well, you needn't worry about that. Arrangements have been made for a bullion van and four plainclothes policemen from the London Bank to meet you at Euston.'

'How shall I know them?'

'They'll know you.'

'When does my responsibility end?'

'You must accompany the bullion to the Bank and wait until it is weighed, then you are clear. After that you can do what you like until next Monday morning when you have to be back here and resume your own work. Now here are three pounds each for your expenses and a pound for incidental expenses of which you must keep a record. We shall all go to the station together and I'll see you off.'

A lorry had drawn up outside. The porters with difficulty lifted the heavy boxes on it and we all sat on top. At the station the boxes were piled neatly into the compartment, between the two sleeping-berths. As the train began to move the head of the Securities Department said, 'Now the responsibility is yours. Good luck.'

Neither of us wanted to sleep; we were much too excited. I had never before been in a first-class carriage; it was thrilling to lie on a comfortable bed on a train rushing south through the darkness, bound for London.

The train stopped for ten minutes in a huge empty station, silent except for a man coming along with a lantern and a hammer with which he struck the wheels or the axles, making the station echo with the clangs. I climbed over the boxes and looked out. In the dim light of the arc lamps I saw the name 'Carlisle'. We were in England.

When dawn broke grey the landscape that sped past us was very different from the Scotland we had left the previous evening. The undulations were much softer, the countryside more intimate, and the trees and foliage sylvan instead of sturdy.

We felt we had entered a foreign land.

As we drew near London more and more little houses dotted the landscape and the stations, through which we slid, became more frequent. Soon walls of dirty brick came up, hemmed us in and passed close; our pace slackened in tunnels and at last we glided to a stop in a vast covered-in atmosphere of soot, smoke, steam and grime—Euston Station. Compared with the Joint Station in Aberdeen it looked huge, but dirty and worn.

Leaving Willox in the compartment with the bullion, I clambered out and stood on the platform, trying my best to assume an air of importance, so that the four plainclothes policemen who were somewhere on the crowded platform would recognise me easily. No one greeted me. The passengers gradually dispersed, leaving on the platform only a few railway men intent on their business. This was strange. I went back to the Guard of the train and asked him if the train were in two sections. 'No sir, just this one.'

I went to Willox seated on the bullion.

'Weren't we told that we would be met by four plainclothes policemen with a bullion van?'

'That's right.'

'Well, there are no policemen here, and no van.'

'That's funny.'

'Where is the gold going? To the Union of London? I seem to remember overhearing someone saying this special consignment was for the Bank of England.'

'I don't know.'

'Let's take it to the Bank of England. I'll try to find a van but first we must get the boxes out of the compartment in case the train is pulled away.'

Two porters laboriously got the boxes on the platform, where they drew the interest of a few draggle-tailed loungers who made remarks to one another in an unknown tongue.

I singled out a railway official, who looked important in a coat with pieces of gold braid on it.

'Where can I get a van to take some luggage across London?'

'What sort of luggage?'

'Twelve heavy boxes.'

He looked along the platform and saw the boxes with the impressive seals.

'What's in them, lead?'

'Yes.'

He threw his glance around. 'Look, there's a van just coming in.' The van he indicated was drawn by two old nags driven by a shabby villainous-looking character.

'Is he all right?'

'Well, you haven't much choice. I don't know when another van will come in.'

I approached the driver who wanted £2. 10*s*. 0*d*. We bargained and finally agreed on £1. 10*s*. 0*d*. The tarpaulin cover of the van was much patched and the floor was worn and splintered, possibly rotten; we loaded the boxes so that the weight was distributed as evenly as possible without putting one on top of another.

We started off at a walking pace, Willox and I seated on the boxes, he spelling out to me the names of the streets, while I checked them off on my map of London to make certain we were being taken towards the Bank of England.

The driver walked his horses all the way until just outside the Bank. Then he used his whip and we charged into the courtyard with urgency and clatter. Gorgeously caparisoned functionaries waved our decrepit equipage to where they wanted it backed against an opening, like a door, high off the ground. Entering this, I was in a wide passage one side of which was a counter. Above the counter was a high screen of thick glass with holes in it. Behind the counter at the nearest hole an official was unlocking drawers. Through the hole I asked him, 'Are you expecting gold today from the North of Scotland Bank, Aberdeen?'

'We are always expecting gold. See if any of those keys fit your boxes.'

He passed me a bunch of keys, one of which unlocked a box. I locked it again and offered him back his keys.

'Yes, one of those keys fits.'

'Well, unlock your boxes, take out the bags, cut the seals and pour the gold through this hole as fast as you can.'

For over three hours I poured gold coins through that hole in the glass on to the counter behind. Two officials shovelled them up as though they were coal and weighed them in bulk. Their scales must have been amazingly accurate as, further along the passage, I heard them demand an extra half-sovereign from a Glasgow consignment.

When the last bagful was weighed the official said, 'Now you're all clear.'

'Thank you, please give me a receipt.'

'A receipt. We don't give receipts.'

This was very unsatisfactory, but I had Willox as a witness that the bullion had been safely delivered.

It was now midday Tuesday. Willox and I discussed what we would do as we had nearly a whole week and London at our disposal. He had, he said, the addresses of several persons whom he intended looking up. I knew of no one and, as I had brought in addition to the £3 from the bank, an extra £3 of my own, I decided to go to Paris. I longed to see the Louvre and the Luxembourg Gallery and I feared this might be the only chance I would ever have. One difficulty would be the language of which I knew only about fifty words and a dozen phrases of village-school French.

If only everything had not happened so unexpectedly I might have had time to get myself prepared.

Trying hard not to be confused by the congested bustling traffic I walked towards London Bridge Station, carefully navigating my way by my map. I gained confidence as, once I got accustomed to the scale, I found that the streets were exactly as they were printed on the map. I memorised part of it and explored the streets of dingy warehouses at both ends of London Bridge.

From London Bridge Station, where I bought a map of Paris, I took the train to Newhaven and crossed by the night boat to Dieppe. I lay down on the way to Paris but sleep was impossible in my excited state. My few words of French were ultimately sufficient to book me a room at a small hotel close to the Gare St Lazare. I left my bag, and started out for the Rive Gauche. Although I had not eaten since the tea and buns of the previous afternoon, I was not hungry but I was very thirsty. The streets were full of men with black eyes, olive skins, and delicate black beards, all of them rather small but very alive and excited.

Something had to be done about my thirst. I sat myself at a marble-topped table outside the most modest café I could find. Sitting at a table right on the street gave me a most uncomfortable feeling. It was as though I were alone on a stage and all the world, including Aberdeen, was watching me critically. A black-coated, white-aproned waiter flicked with a napkin the top of the table and muttered unintelligibly.

I wanted a long drink, not a stimulant, but had no idea as to what to order. Did the French drink anything besides wine?

He jabbered again and I became embarrassed.

'Quelque—chose—pour—boire.'

He became now really excited, but I did not get one word of what he said. I shook my head. With a resigned air he shrugged his shoulders and turned into the café. I resolved to wait five minutes.

He returned with a bottle and a glass, drew the cork and left me. The stuff had a curious flavour, bitter and warming, but at least it was wet. I was so thirsty I drank it up as though it were water. I felt I was drawing impertinent glances from the other waiters so I paid and, consulting my map, started off for the Luxembourg.

Although I was walking uphill, the street glided smoothly past as though I were on silken wheels and going down-hill—a most curious sensation. The door of the Luxembourg Gallery swerved before it stood in front of me. Inside I recognised immediately Whistler's portrait of his mother, but it kept receding from me first on one side then on the other—this in spite of my efforts to get it to remain steady in front of me. Suddenly I realised to my horror that the wine had affected my balance. I made a dead straight line to a bench a few yards away and reached it safely.

I sat on that bench for probably an hour or two until things began to steady themselves, periodically making test journeys to different pictures. I remained in the gallery till closing time, studying the paintings of the impressionists, particularly what was to be seen of Manet's work.

After a meal at a nearby café I walked slowly back towards my hotel savouring the life of the streets, feeling strangely at ease and irresponsible, as though I had been denuded of the heavy armour of respectability.

My way back took me past the opera house. The placards at the door showed that Richard Wagner's *Valkyrie* was being performed. I bought a ticket for the gallery, but when I had climbed all the way up, there was not a seat available. Along with many others, I stood on the stairs that led still higher. A multitude of heads sloped down precipitously to a gap beyond which, in the far distance, was a small stage, on which the performers seemed like dolls viewed through the wrong end of a telescope.

After fifteen minutes I caught myself falling asleep; I sweated when I imagined what would have happened had I lost my balance and gone head foremost down into the dark sounding cavern yawning at my feet; I had no papers or passport upon me whereby I could be identified. Willox, in London, alone knew I intended to go to Paris. Aberdeen seemed centuries away—a dim memory from a former existence.

I realised that I had not had one minute's sleep since early Monday morning and it was now late on Wednesday night. I jammed a finger tightly into the ornamental ironwork beneath the stair rail at my side. Several times I fell asleep but the moment I began to sway my finger woke me.

By midnight I had reached my hotel safely by consulting my map. The little money I had did not warrant my taking a cab.

After a sound sleep I was at the Louvre early and spent the whole of that day in the gallery, taking the night boat back to London via Dieppe–Newhaven.

Friday I spent in the National Gallery, Saturday wandering about London on foot. Willox and I met as arranged and journeyed north together, reaching Aberdeen on Sunday morning.

After a few hours under the cold grey sky of Aberdeen, Paris and London were but the precious memories of a dream.

VI

At home a cheerful atmosphere became habitual. In the morning I rose, made up and lit the fire, and in twenty minutes my grandmother had cooked the porridge for our breakfast. First she added salt to the boiling water, then she stirred in gradually the raw oatmeal until the mess became thickish. She then poured all out on our plates, where they set firm, and sprinkled raw oatmeal on top to make them attractive. This retained their 'smeddum'-imparting quality, she maintained.* She had a contempt for the 'oatmeal soup' which appealed to the 'Englified'. She had a high tea ready for me at 5 p.m. when I got home from the bank. The shopping was easy; on my way to the bank I ordered from the shops what she required for our simple wants.

Happy months passed thus; but on my return one afternoon I found her on the floor, uninjured, cheerful, but unable to get up. She had, she said, become dizzy and had fallen about an hour previously. Alarmed, I questioned her and learned that she had fallen many times, but luckily had always managed to get up unassisted.

She treated the whole affair as a bothersome trifle but I had to take a more serious view. In my imagination, I saw her falling and striking her head on the fender or on

* 'Smeddum' means energy. McBey maintained that in Scotland the porridge was always alluded to in the plural.

a chair, injuring herself. I suggested asking one or perhaps two of the neighbours to look in occasionally, but this she would not have.

At the bank I became increasingly anxious, not knowing what I might find when I reached home, and finally discussed the problem with her eldest son Willie. The fact had to be faced that to pay anyone to come and look after her during the day would mean using up her small capital, as my salary was just about enough to keep body and soul together in the two of us. Also we knew she would have resented any implication that she was failing, although she was now 89 years old.

Finally, it was agreed that Willie would take her to live with him and his wife and two sons. When she learned of this she was most unwilling to consent, but finally gave in on my telling her that I would be all right in lodgings and that I would come out the two miles to visit her on Sunday afternoons.

Our home was broken up, the few pieces of furniture dispersed, and I took her and her few belongings to the home of her son. A numb sadness came on me at parting with the one being in the world who was dear to me. She had in the last three years made my home life a happy one.

To take her mind off the separation, in case she would feel it as I did, I engaged for the journey one of the newly installed horseless cabs. She had never been in a railway carriage even, and was so tickled at being pulled along the streets by a little coughing engine, that she settled down easily in her new home.

I found myself lodgings—a room high up in an office building in Union Street, with as landlady Mrs Barclay, the wife of the caretaker. Three other young men each had a room on the same floor, one of them, Willie by name, had a job connected with Robert Gordon's College, but the occupations of the other two were not disclosed.

Mrs Barclay was a thin, pale, harassed woman, with large light credulous eyes, wispy flaxen hair, and a gentle disposition. She and her daughter, a simple buxom girl, did their best to cater for her lodgers and, on the whole, meant well. Together they had worked out the type and time of meals most suited to their mutual convenience and purses. Every Sunday at one o'clock an enormous treacle dumpling resembling a large pale football was served. On this soggy mass the three lodgers so gorged themselves that they had no interest in food until the following Tuesday evening, when the usual high tea again commenced.

This arrangement struck me as unusual, but as the address was convenient for both the bank and my 'studio', and none of the lodgers appeared to suffer from indigestion, I agreed to conform to the reptilian custom already established.

To be relieved of all domestic worries was a great change for me and the one-family-like atmosphere of my lodgings had its amusing side. One Friday morning there was a sharp pain in my chest when I breathed. A doctor was called, who diagnosed it as pleurisy and instructed me to remain in bed and get my landlady to put a poultice on my left side. Mrs Barclay made one and put it on me so hot that it burnt me right round from my breast to my back bone.

Next day when the doctor came he saw the inflammation was no better, and, not noticing that the poultice had burnt me, instructed Mrs Barclay to paint on iodine. This treatment was so painful that in agony I grasped so tensely two of the upright brass pillars at the head of my bed that I unwittingly pulled my head through between them.

They held me by the neck in such a way that it was impossible to extricate my head. Pillows had to be piled on a chair at the top of my bed so that my head could be supported until two of my fellow lodgers might come home and pull aside the bars sufficiently to free me.

Before they could return, whilst I was still held a prisoner by the head bars of my bed and in pain, the Aberdeen representative of a Dundee newspaper came to my room to furnish me with a subject for the usual weekly cartoon. That week he had what he believed to be a pungent and witty idea. My appreciation of it was, perforce, muted. The situation did appeal to him as somewhat incongruous.

In five days I was back working in the bank. On the Sunday I went to visit my grandmother, hoping she had not noticed I had missed a Sunday. Scarcely had I been seated when she asked, 'Why didn't you come to see me last Sunday?'

'It was such a day of storm and sleet; I would have been soaked to the skin.'

She appeared satisfied with my excuse and placidly continued knitting, but an hour later, when we were alone for a few minutes, she asked me without warning, 'Last Sunday at this time you were lying in your bed and a woman was bending over you doing something to your left side; who was she?'

'You must have fallen asleep and dreamt all this.'

She ignored completely my attempt to mislead her and persisted, 'Who was that woman, and what was she doing to you?'

Further concealment of my illness was useless. I told her all. To me her faculty in the realm of the supernatural had many times been uncanny and I ought to have known better than to attempt to deceive her.

She appeared to be happy in her new home. Now that she was settled comfortably I began to consider seriously my leaving the bank for good.

I had worked hard for eleven years and in that period had been paid exactly £497. 10s. 0d. I was now earning a salary of £80 per annum and although I rendered to the bank the industry, the loyalty, and the efficiency it expected, I had no real interest in the work, nor did I seek to improve whatever prospects of advancement I may have had by sitting for the examinations of the Banker's Institute, which appeared formidable to me but which my fellow clerks passed with ease.

In the vista of the future I saw myself as the defenceless victim of the whims and jealousies of my superiors, holding precariously a position of dour respectability. By the unremitting exercise of strict thrift I could keep myself alive on a miserable salary, but in a constant state of anxiety lest by an involuntary slip or an error of judgement I might endanger both my chances of advancement and, at the tail end of a lifetime of faithful subservience, a small pension.

I had not the slightest cause to imagine I might be able to earn a livelihood as an artist, but to founder quickly on the high seas appealed to me as a better fate than to decay slowly in harbour.

I had my capital of £200, which I calculated was sufficient to last me for two years, probably with care a little more.

I decided to cut adrift from the bank, and gave the two months' obligatory notice, which was received without comment. I did not expect any expressions of regret; I knew well that I could be replaced by a clerk earning an even smaller salary than mine.

As the time for my leaving drew near I was curious to know what would happen and asked for letters of recommendation from the manager, the secretary, the accountant, and the chief inspector; each gave me a written tribute, which in the circumstances was couched in terms of such praise that I felt there must be a mistake or a catch somewhere.

For my last ten days in the bank's service I was given an understudy, who, when I left, would be able to carry on the work of the stationery desk without a jolt. I introduced him to all the firms from whom I had purchased supplies, acquainting him with their little foibles and jealousies. I primed him as to who could be trusted and who had to be watched, but as an ethical compensation to my superiors for the wonderful letters of recommendation they had given me, I refrained from showing him how to make his books balance exactly without the accompaniment of headaches, eye-strain, nights of late work, and risk of detection.

I had considered carefully my plans for my immediate future. I could not, somehow, face the prospect of terminating eleven years in a secure if humble situation and then falling suddenly, the very next day, in much the same environment, into relative idleness. The break had to be accentuated somehow, so I decided to sail to Amsterdam— the city where Rembrandt lived and worked.

My last day in the bank fell on a Saturday, the 10th of July 1910. At 12.45 I handed my keys to my successor, wished him luck, and took a last look round the imposing marble and mahogany hive of industry. Involuntarily I reflected that although at the moment it might appear a prison, I might some day wistfully look back on it as having been a refuge, the security of which I had not appreciated.

Everyone was much too busy to waste time bidding good-bye so at 1.10 p.m. I quietly walked out.

Although McBey did his best to make the end of his career at the bank a complete break, his Aberdeen roots were not to be instantly broken. There was an interval when he set about establishing himself in his new profession in the familiar surroundings which, if not welcoming to his amateur work, had at least provided all the encouragement he had so far received. But immediately his mind was bent on Holland, for which he was bound the very day that he left the bank.

That same evening I sailed on board the *St Sunniva*, bound for Leith. At Leith I transhipped to a small cargo steamer in which I was the only passenger. She carried on her well-deck, forward of the bridge, a dense throng of worn-out horses tethered to ropes running fore and aft. From the south-west came a gale that made the vessel pitch and roll so badly that the tightly wedged horses, scrambling for balance, tangled their tethers to such an extent that the ones pinned in the alleyways could not be reached by their two attendants.

It was a pathetic sight. I spent most of the voyage in a deck chair on the windy exposed bridge feeling that, so long as I was in the open air, I might not be seasick. It was a relief when, after two days and nights, we reached Ijmuiden, and in the grey of the morning cleared the lock gates and slowly entered the Ijmuiden canal. I had not eaten on the way across but now I had a good hasty breakfast and climbed on deck.

Floating high above the surrounding countryside we glided gently up the canal. It was entrancing, from the vantage position of the steamer's bridge, to gaze down on what seemed the whole of Holland, spread out like a vast green painted floor that stretched flat to the level horizon in every direction. The small farms and the distant windmills resembled ships becalmed on a lush green ocean. Soon, in the grey distance, the church spires of Amsterdam serrated the base line of the sky; as we neared the city quaint craft, strangely rigged, sailed and tacked all about us. Except for the anachronous presence of a steamship here and there we might have been entering the eighteenth century. A tug nosed us gently alongside a quay.

Soon steam was in the winches and our deck cargo of old horses was slung ashore, one by one, some of them hardly able to stand up. During the voyage seven or eight had died, stiffened and become jammed in the alleyways, so presenting to the crew a problem in unloading. Ultimately the wire cable was noosed around the neck of each of those horses and the animal pulled out forcibly and slung high in the air on its way to the quayside. A crowd of Dutchmen each with wooden clogs on his feet and a cigar in his mouth stood and watched the proceedings with intense curiosity.

The fascinating city and shipping of Amsterdam formed an incongruous background for the unpleasant spectacle of a dead horse with a strangely elongated neck swaying against the sky.

Leaving my bag, paint box, and cycle on the steamer, I landed and by the aid of a map of the streets made my way to the address of the minister of the Scottish Church, to whom I had a note of introduction given me by a friend in the bank. I asked him if he knew where I might get lodgings with a Dutch family. He came with me to the home of a widow by the name of Kamp in the Bosboom Toussain Straat. The younger of her two sons, of about my own age, was the agent for Bibby's oil cake for cattle and spoke English perfectly.

As his time was his own and he also had a cycle, he suggested that on the morrow we would together go for a thirty-mile run in the country north of Amsterdam, taking sandwiches with us.

The next day the sun shone between bold white clouds. We crossed the Ij by ferry and cycled north amongst the windmills of Zaandam all busily turning their arms in the fresh breeze.

At noon we paused at the hamlet of Wijde Wormer, and rested in a field of thick lush grass in the lee of a copse. Between the friendly stalks of hay close to my eyes the tiny windmills in the far distance spun their sails briskly in the sunshine.

From a neighbouring field the strong smell of newly mown hay scented the air. Near us towered, like a thatched castle, an old windmill; the creaking swish made by each huge arm as it swept past its nadir on its way to the white clouds overhead was as music to me, lying relaxed on my back sunk deep in the rich and juicy green, luxuriating in my newly-won sense of freedom.

The five days that had elapsed since I slipped from the shackles of the bank had been so full of incident that I had no opportunity to lie back and savour my happiness. In the hour I rested at Wijde Wormer many harsh memories of the past eleven years were softened. I thanked Providence.

In the afternoon we cycled to Volendam. I had never seen an artist at work till now; here were artists working in the open and unashamed.

Before recrossing the Ij at Amsterdam we sat for an hour on the bank entranced by the busy shipping on the broad expanse of water silhouetted against the setting sun. I knew that this day would stay in my memory and fell to wondering if more such days would be granted me in the next two years.

With my map, a 16″ × 12″ oil colour box, sketchbook and stool, I wandered about the streets and canals of Amsterdam, working whenever weather and circumstances permitted. I went to trouble to ensconce myself in a doorway or on a moored barge, as invariably I became self-conscious and embarrassed when unmannerly idlers slunk towards me, rooted themselves behind me, breathed on the back of my neck and watched stolidly every stroke of my brush and every little move I made.

When the weather was inclement, I spent the time in the Rijksmuseum, studying intensely the paintings and etchings of Rembrandt, whose 'Night Watch', hanging alone in a special chamber, imposingly separated from the public by a barrier and guards, was the show-piece of the museum. I was more impressed by his 'Syndics of the Drapers' Guild' which was hung in a good side light in one of the very small rooms; as it was not fenced off one could study with a fascinating intimacy the sure authoritative handling of the paint and guess at the number and colour of the glazes employed to produce the amazing illusion of depth.

Although it chanced I was often in that small room with no other person being present, I never did feel alone. It was uncanny. Those fine Dutch burghers had paused in their deliberations and were watching me, a chance intruder, from their frame. They had, with patient tolerance, watched intruders for 250 years.

All the authors of the books on Art in the Aberdeen Library, with the exception of Ruskin, had prepared me to be impressed by the works of Rembrandt and I reacted immediately now that I saw them at first-hand. These same authors had mentioned Frans Hals almost with faint disparagement as a painter for whom excuses ought to be made; that, although he was not of the same class as Raphael, Rembrandt, Titian, Veronese, or Leonardo da Vinci, he could not be completely overlooked.

I was endeavouring to form in my mind a hierarchy of painters, but my studies had been confused by a publication *The Hundred Best Painters* which came in twenty-four parts containing six sepia reproductions in each. It had all the hallmarks of authority and erudition but included 'The Knight Errant' by Sir John Millais, P.R.A., 'The Symbol' by Frank Dicksee, R.A., 'The Catapult' by Lord Leighton, P.R.A., 'The Last Muster' by Herbert von Herkomer, R.A., and 'The Sculptor's Studio' by Sir L. Alma-Tadema, R.A.

Now as I stood, fascinated, in front of Hals's 'The Fool' and 'Man with a Wine Glass', the omission of those from the 'Hundred Best Painters' confused me still further. The fool, a lad in motley playing a guitar, and the man with a big black hat holding a glass were alive; and painted with an ease and assurance which seemed incredible. Although the paint was thin, the pictures were so well preserved that they might have been painted the previous week.

I could not rest until I had made a journey to Haarlem and treated myself to a memorable day in the Frans Hals Museum.

Always on the look-out for antique blank paper on which to print my etchings, I haunted the old book shops on the quays, purchasing a few fly leaves here and a few there. Whilst prowling one lucky morning in the flea-market in the Waterlooplein near the Jewish quarter, I saw, half submerged amongst a clutter of old books and papers dumped on the pavement, a brown leather-bound volume about 30" × 27". It contained 100 leaves of blank paper the like of which I had never seen, all in good condition, most of them with tiny squares of old paper still attached here and there. High on the outside front binding was stamped in gold the one word 'Rubens' with, near it, a many-pronged star. On the back binding was also stamped in gold '31' and the date 1637. Unquestionably all genuine and of the period.

I bargained with its owner, an old man, black-bearded, Jewish, and bought it for 12 guilders, about £1 sterling. Years afterwards I found it had belonged to Rembrandt, who probably kept in it drawings by, or engravings of the paintings of Rubens. The small pieces of old paper still attached to the leaves were part of the hinged mounts which held the engravings in place and, like enough, had been gummed on by Rembrandt himself; perhaps by Saskia; perhaps by Hendrickje Stoffels.

The two parallel islands that, in the old part of the city, formed the Jewish Quarter became one of my favourite sketching grounds, and I began to know it well. I was even allowed, for a small fee, to sketch diamond polishers

at work. I was amazed at the skill with which, using only
their naked fingers, they set a tiny diamond in the apex
of a cone of molten lead and antimony so that when the
lead became cold it could be held inverted on the spinning
polishing wheel to get a new facet.

The picturesque squalor of the streets in the quarter lent
itself as a subject for etching, but I had brought no copper
plates because of their weight and the extreme delicacy of the
wax ground. I made many pencil sketches, but the medium
was not very satisfactory. I wanted to use a line as precise as
a hard pencil would give, but with more freedom than was
possible with such a tool.

When my landlady, Mrs Kamp, learned that I was in
the habit of frequenting the Jewish Quarter she was most
perturbed and, through her English-speaking son, implored
me not to enter the quarter again. As no one had shown
hostility towards me I was even more amazed when I learned
that none of the Kamp family had ever been in the Jewish
Quarter, because they regarded it as unsafe for Christians to
venture there.

The Kamp household evidently held themselves responsible for my safety, so, as I intended to go to North Holland
for a spell, I gave the promise the old lady wanted for the
sake of the family's peace of mind.

For sketching in North Holland, the village of Volendam
seemed the best base. There, right on the harbour, was the
English-speaking Spaander Hotel which, moreover, had a
special weekly rate for artists—an important consideration. I
tied my sketching gear and my bag on my cycle and leisurely
made my way by the route Jan Kamp and I had followed six
weeks previously. I engaged a room which, with food, was
to cost 30s. a week.

I found myself one of about sixty guests of all nationalities,
most of them artists, who at meals seated themselves at two
long parallel tables in the dining-room. The dishes of food
were passed along by the guests, all helping themselves. I
took an empty chair on the right of a thin, elderly, spry,
clean-shaven man who told me he was an American artist.

The dishes came along from his left and soon I, on his right, noticed that no dish passed him. He emptied it every time, and I had always to wait for the next refill. The amount of food he devoured was to me, a frugal eater, amazing. At the end of the meal he remarked dryly, 'You will no doubt have observed that I am a bad man to follow. Everybody avoids the seat you are in.' He was the first American I had met, and I wondered if all Americans had his astonishing capacity for food.

With Volendam as a centre, I cycled to the neighbouring villages with my sketching outfit. Before setting out one morning I went to the counter in the hotel where art materials were sold, to get a new pencil.

Alida Spaander had no pencils in stock, but suggested that I used her fountain pen till such time as she got a new supply of pencils. I took the pen; it was at least better than nothing. I cycled to Monnickendam and started a small drawing of trees with the old square tower of the church showing between them. To my delight the easily flowing precise ink line which the pen made was the perfect medium for the record I wanted, far more satisfactory than pencil. I borrowed Alida's pen every day for the rest of my fortnight's stay on Volendam, and bought two in Amsterdam the first day of my return to that city.

On 8 September 1910 I sailed back to Leith and four days later arrived back under the grey sky of Aberdeen with a score of small oil paintings and two sketchbooks filled with my pen drawings.

I had taken as a studio a small room with a top light in a building recently erected at 25 Crown Street. There I worked hard all the autumn and winter making etchings of Dutch subjects based on my pen-and-ink drawings. Several of them seemed good to me, but I began to feel anxious because, since the day I left the bank in July, I had not sold even one painting or print.

In the city of Aberdeen were seven or eight artists, each of whom seemed able to earn a professional livelihood, perhaps supplemented by teaching, or family connections.

The Art Gallery had six years previously been extended at great expense to the accompaniment of considerable fanfaronade and acclamation. The Art Gallery Committee of eighteen, appointed by the Town Council, balked at purchasing the work of local artists, although the previous year they had parted with £700 for a painting by Edward Stott, A.R.A., entitled 'The Flight'—a twilighty sentimental rendering of Joseph and Mary, who held in her arms a glowing bundle, and the ass. Joseph, curiously enough, was depicted as a bent old man with a scraggy white beard wearing a dressing-gown and vague trousers. The ass, bearing Mary seated side saddle, was stepping out bravely but alongside it poor old Joseph appeared to be staggering in the last throes of exhaustion. Truly a strange choice made, on behalf of the city, by a committee of hard-headed, matter-of-fact Aberdonians.

I was well aware that the individual Aberdonian, reared to husband his resources, spent cannily, even apprehensively, and I realised that I could never make a livelihood in the city I knew so well. The arts of bluff and salesmanship were beyond me, and the hawking of my work repugnant. Nevertheless something had to be done unless I were to disintegrate slowly in the full sight of my late co-workers in the bank, so I resolved that, unless a stroke of luck came my way soon, I would emigrate to London.

Recalling that someone in Glasgow had bought two of my etchings—the only sale I had ever made—I mounted two sets of my prints, about eighteen in each, and took them to Aitken Dott & Son in Edinburgh. George Proudfoot, sole partner of the firm, examined them seriously but said there was no market in Edinburgh for etchings and advised me to try London. On my asking him for advice as to how to do this he wrote on an envelope R. L. Milne, Manager, Goupil & Co., Bedford Street, Strand, and advised me to write to that firm. At his suggestion I left five prints of Dutch subjects with Aitken Dott 'on sale' at 31s. 6d. each.

The same day I crossed to Glasgow and took my bundle to the firm of Messrs Connell. One of the partners glanced hastily at the etchings and said, 'They're all right, but not the kind of work we handle. Come back when you have done something really important.'

This was not encouraging.

Next I took them to George Davidson Ltd in their Sauchiehall Street Galleries. George Davidson examined them at length, asked which firms had already seen them, and said, 'Your prints are good. We might be able to work up a market for them in time. Meantime, leave with us on sale or return the eleven I have put separately and we shall do what we can at 33¹⁄₃ per cent commission.'

I returned to Aberdeen, somewhat discouraged at not having sold a single print, but at least I had a dim hope of Edinburgh and Glasgow as potential markets and I felt a slight comfort in that my work had been regarded seriously by two dealers, Proudfoot and Davidson.

I wrote to London, but sending no prints, asking Goupil & Co. if they would be willing to take my etchings for sale and what their terms were. They replied they would be glad to take my work 'on sale or return' at a commission for themselves of 66²⁄₃ per cent on all sales. Although I thought these terms somewhat one-sided and greedy I agreed; I wanted my work shown in London; I was in no position to bargain and I had noticed that no period of duration was specified in their letter. I sent them a parcel of thirty different prints.

In February I had a stroke of luck: a Mrs W. R. Macdonell, whom I had heard of as a woman of culture who was interested in art, asked Lindsay Smith, the artist who was painting her portrait, to take her to my studio. A few days later she returned with her husband, and bought nine of my prints at my own figure—£14. 3s. 6d.

Happening to glance at the advertisements in the London *Studio*, a monthly publication, I came across in the December 1910 issue a notice, 'charming studio to let, top light, side light, service inclusive £40 per annum. Mrs. Schupp, 8 Wharfedale Street, Redcliffe Square, London, S.W.' Acting on an impulse, I wrote Mrs Schupp that if her studio were still unlet I would take it for a year from 1st June, as the tenancy of my studio in Crown Street, Aberdeen, expired at the end of May. Mrs Schupp agreed to this, and, quietly, I began my preparations to leave Aberdeen.

Now that my decision was made I had a feeling of relief and a comfortable indifference regarding my complete failure to make headway in Aberdeen, so much so that I took steps to have a 'one-man' exhibition of my etchings before I went south.

In the whole city there was but one gallery where an artist could show serious work. The others relied mostly on over-the-counter business in reproductions of popular paintings and the sale of art materials for 'lady amateurs'.

The Gallery of John Kesson was a small, dark, obscure workshop in Diamond Street, with a small, bare, fairly well-lit room above. The old man was skilled in the making and gilding of frames to which he gave his whole time. Willie Gallow, his manager, who ran the business, was supposed to be the trusted art adviser to the more affluent Aberdonians; and had the reputation of being an able salesman for several of the local artists on the infrequent occasions when a picture was wanted. Willie had a long, thin face, smooth, ruddy skin, appraising brown eyes and a thin, dark moustache with dropping tusk-like ends. His deportment was cautious and smoothly confidential. Business was discussed in undertones over whiskies at the near-by bar of the Grand Hotel, there being no facilities, even a chair, at the Gallery.

I approached him regarding his terms for an exhibition of from twenty to thirty of my etchings. At first his attitude was aloof and condescending, but, anticipating this, I was careful to listen with deference and foment his assurance instead of betraying resentment, with the result that, after several whiskies, he was willing to have a three-day exhibition of my etchings, no charge to be made for the Gallery. I was to pay for the mounts, the catalogues, the invitations, and the press announcements, his commission on sales to be one third of the selling price.

I had, somehow, no expectation that the exhibition would be at all successful, although I did hope that I would not actually be out-of-pocket after I had paid the expenses. Gallow had advised me that it was not usual for an artist to attend his own exhibition; I was relieved not to have to be at the Gallery on the exhibition days—3, 4, and 5 May 1911.

After it closed, he assured me that invitations had been sent to all the patrons of art in the city, that most of them had been to the Gallery but the result was disappointing, as of the twenty-five prints exhibited only five had been sold. My share of the proceeds barely covered my expenses.

Had I expected my exhibition to be a success, even to a small extent, I would have felt despondent and discouraged at its complete failure; now, on the contrary, my reaction was that the wisdom of my decision to quit Aberdeen had been put to the test and it was more than justified by results.

In the last three months Goupil's in London had managed to dispose of about a dozen etchings. Although the proceeds remitted to me by them—one third of the selling price— were small, the fact that they could sell any at all was not without significance.

By 28 May 1911, the date on which the tenancy of my Crown Street studio expired, I had ready for shipment by the London Steamer my dismantled printing press, two cases of paper, two small tables, two chairs, one portmanteau and a cycle—total cost for shipment to London £4. 13s. 8d.

On my way to bid goodbye to my grandmother I kept suppressing the gnawing fear that I might never see her again, but she took leave of me with such happy unconcern, as if her gift of clairvoyance made her secretly confident that she would see me again soon.

Travelling south by train, I broke the journey at Stirling to pick up several etchings I had sent to a print-seller in the town. I walked up to the castle and from the ramparts watched the sun disappear in a golden blaze behind the distant mountains. In the darkening afterglow I bade goodbye to Scotland, a fair but stern land that held for me sad associations, and in whose rigid economy I, as an artist, had no place.

As I turned and retraced my steps southwards to the station I sensed that my adventure to London and into the unknown had from that moment commenced.

Epilogue

'Spent the day unpacking. Felt dreadfully weary or homesick, I do not know which. Sight of my poor little possessions upset me completely', runs the entry in McBey's diary soon after his arrival in London at the end of May 1911. Work was the best but only a partial cure for misery. Although his friend Lindsay Smith, the artist, took him to the Chelsea Arts Club, he remained lonely. In July he decided to visit Spain (the fare was £5. 19s. 0d.) with a young artist, D. I. Smart. There he saw his first bull-fight, and the Velasquez room at the Prado to which he returned again and again. From dawn to dusk he was busy sketching; he developed a lasting passion for the Spanish landscape. Money ran short and he and Smart were obliged to sleep out, but it was a cholera epidemic that finally drove them home in September. McBey settled down to work for the exhibition that Goupil's had agreed to put on in November. Altogether, he made 20 plates, including a sequence of 7 drypoints of a bull-fight, among them some of his most powerful prints: *The Ovation to the Matador*, *The Banderillas*, and *A Fierce Bull*.

'Few attended', he wrote in his diary on the first day, 21 November. If so, that was the only suggestion of failure about it. Two days later Goupil's had sold 29 prints, and 77 by 6 December. The press was uniformly enthusiastic: 'An etcher new to us,' wrote the art critic of the *Morning Post*, 'and we are prepared to follow him on the long way he is sure to go.' London became a more cheerful place. He went often to the Chelsea Arts Club, where he met William Hutcheon, who was on the *Morning Post*, and Martin Hardie, Keeper of Prints and Drawings at the Victoria and Albert Museum.*

* Author of *Etchings and Drypoints from* 1902 *to* 1924 *by James McBey*, London, 1925.

Both remained firm friends and supporters for life. At the same time, Hardie was inadvertently responsible for a rebuff which coloured the rest of McBey's life. He urged him to send his work and apply for election as an associate of the Royal Society of Painter-Etchers and Engravers. He did, but was not elected, and this (with the rejection of his work a year later by the Royal Academy) decided him to be independent of all societies and go his own way. He was hurt but not resentful. Later when both societies invited him to join them, he politely refused.

Christmas and New Year were spent in Aberdeen. On the way back, he stopped at Glasgow to see George Davidson, who wanted to hold an exhibition of his work. Goupil's objected, and this precipitated the break which the terms of their contract had made inevitable. The Glasgow exhibition, held in February 1912, was an equal success: 89 prints were sold in a week, and sales continued steadily. Other art dealers took an interest in his work and soon McBey found himself represented, on much more satisfactory terms than Goupil's, by Colnaghi. (As a result, Aitken Dott held an exhibition of his prints in January 1913, and Knoedler in America in October 1914.) He met Malcolm Salaman, the leading authority on prints in his time, who was to write a monograph on McBey's work.* He discovered the delights of the Kentish landscape with another artist, J. Kerr Lawson, of whom he became very fond, and spent his summer holiday back at Aberdeen, sketching scenes of his childhood.

In the winter of 1912 he and Kerr Lawson decided on a joint trip to Morocco. They first went to Tetuan. McBey was wholly captivated by the landscape, people, and the way of life. It was a love which lasted until his death. They lodged in the Soko, the old citadel of the town, and, as in Spain, they drew and painted throughout the daylight hours. In the process, McBey made another accidental discovery of medium, which again radically changed his methods of work.

* *The Etchings of James McBey*, London, 1929.

As I was leaving the house for Morocco, a bottle of oil, which was insecure in my sketching bag, needed wedging, and I seized the first object that came to hand. This happened to be a palette for watercolours; and although I had no intention of working in wash, when in Morocco, I found it very fascinating to put colour over my pen drawing. This is how I came to produce watercolour drawings.

He painted the narrow winding alleys, the doorways, the markets, the landscape round Tetuan, and (not without danger in an Arab country) the people themselves. On 5 January Kerr Lawson went home, and McBey decided to go to Tangier, then a difficult and even dangerous journey. But first he paid a private farewell to Tetuan: 'Took walk by river in the afternoon and at seven minutes to four plucked flower at point farthest from home I have ever been.' It became a lifelong custom, before leaving a place that had affected him deeply, to pick a flower or leaf and note it in his diary. Later he made some notably poetic etchings based on his Tetuan sketches: *The Story Teller, The Orange Seller, Beggars*, and *Gunsmiths* show how completely the atmosphere of the place possessed him. Now he crossed the hills and mountains to Tangier, travelling part of the way at night to avoid brigands. First impressions were recorded in a beautiful mysterious plate, *Tangier*, of the town at sunset, a caravan of Arabs on donkeys riding along the pale empty beach. He visited an English friend who lived in a house, El Foolk, on the Old Mountain overlooking the bay. It was in that house, forty-five years later, that he died.

The year 1914 was one of outstanding accomplishment for McBey. Light, weather, and atmospherics, as well as a notable sense of space and distance, were embodied in a number of plates: *The Lion Brewery* and *The Pool*, both studies of the Thames, and three plates showing scenes along the Scottish coast—*Sea and Rain, Macduff: The Moray Firth,* and *Gamrie*. Back in London, he returned to a life now busy and social. He travelled about, to East Anglia (the source of his beautiful etching, *Night at Ely Cathedral*) and back to Scotland. He received his first portrait commission, and he bought two Rembrandt etchings. He had not thought of his watercolours as more than sketches, but Colnaghi's saw their merits, rescued them from neglect on the studio floor, and held a highly successful exhibition of them in February 1914. In the same month McBey left Wharfedale Street and took a lease of William Rothenstein's studio in Oak Hill Park, Hampstead, where he remained till he went into the army. The early days of the war were punctuated by an unhappy love affair, and by the death of his father, whom he had met again as a prosperous sheep-farmer at Warlingham in Surrey; his father made him his executor and left him £1,000, but the will was complicated and he refused both legacy and executorship.

In November 1915 he heard of the death of his grand-mother at the age of 95. 'Felt dull blow—terribly sad—frightened.' He left immediately for Newburgh. 'Poor old girl,' he wrote in his diary, 'would have liked to have been holding her hand when she went. She looked beautiful—not more than 50—her skin transparent and her little hands just as I knew them so well. The only friend I have ever had. Funeral—to churchyard in motors. Only about 10 there. There were no flowers. Buried simply, as she had lived. I lowered her left side. On quiet days she may hear the anvil at the Smithy.' A few years before his own death, the portrait that he had painted of her in 1901, his first ever, was returned to him, and he found, still wedged between the canvas and the stretcher, the sealed note he had placed there when he painted it, inscribed 'Whoever finds this please communicate with James McBey if still alive.' The note ran:

> Saturday, 24 March, 1901.
> 42 Union Grove, Aberdeen.

To All whom it may concern,

A week ago I finished my first portrait '*Mam*', it was begun on the 22nd of January, the day of the Queen's funeral. I have started one of Jas. D. Davidson accountant in the Bank to which I have the misfortune to belong for another three years, as I was two years in it on 15th. God only knows what I shall do when I leave it, for this is a queer world.

James McBey

After several rejections, due to his bad eyesight, he was commissioned in January 1916 as a Second Lieutenant and sent to Army Printing and Stationery Services at Boulogne, a secret but unexciting job. It was a more serious matter that sketching was against regulations: Martin Hardie has recorded how these were circumvented.

McBey's *Quai Gambetta* was done easily and without subterfuge from the window of our upper room. Eagerly I watched every line of it drawn on the plate in the acid bath. For other subjects—*A Norman Port, The Crucifix, Boulogne*, and *The Sussex*—McBey had to depend on thumbnail notes, and on small sketches made in the palm of the hand, and even inside his pocket. It was on *The Sussex*—the torpedoed passenger steamship, with the forward part of her blown away, yet miraculously beached close to Boulogne—that the artist concentrated his efforts. Night after night he went to look at her tragic hull, and gradually, after making endless local notes and composition studies at home, he evolved what is one of the noblest, most spiritual of his plates. Where another might have made the scene with the setting sun behind the tortured wreck, flamboyant and spectacular, McBey was content to give a subtle, restrained impression, at once solemn and beautiful, strangely moving in its effect.*

His work also took him to Le Havre, and from there he walked to Harfleur, where he visited the Schneider munition works. This was the source of *France at her Furnaces*, one of the most famous of his war-time etchings. In February 1917 he spent a week's leave on the Somme, travelling from Étaples to Meaulte, where he came under fire and slept

---

* Martin Hardie, *Etchings and Drypoints from* 1902 *to* 1924 *by James McBey*, London, 1925, p. xv.

in a dug-out, and back to Abbeville. The five etchings which resulted from this period epitomised the destruction, desolation, and tragedy on the Western front.

In March, a change came. Campbell Dodgson, Keeper of Prints and Drawings at the British Museum, recommended him for appointment as Official War Artist with the British Expeditionary Force under Allenby in Egypt. He sailed on 26 May 1917, and on reaching Cairo started work with his usual vigour and enthusiasm. He got up at 5 daily to work before the heat became too intense, and continued until nightfall. He drew Cairo, Ismailia, the desert, the Port Said docks, prisoner-of-war and Armenian refugee camps, travelling as best he could, by foot, in canal boats, in an open railway truck, eating whenever he got a chance ('plate of onions at 6 p.m.'). He went on a five-day reconnaissance into the Sinai desert with the Australian Camel Patrol, when he made the drawing on which one of his best-known etchings, *Dawn: The Camel Patrol Setting Out*, was based.

Despite the violent heat of June and July, he completed no less than thirty-five finished drawings, which he sent home. While in Cairo he had a brief but intense love affair with an English woman, the wife of a government official, who foretold that the Arab world would have a profound effect on his work. When he left for the front in Palestine, she saw him off at the station; 'a white figure', he wrote in his diary, 'passes out of my life forever'.

With Allenby's army he was a member of the Press Camp and Mess, along with war correspondents and the 'official cinematographer', but this did not solve the transport problem, always difficult in a campaign of rapid movement. He missed the fall of Gaza, but arrived in Jerusalem on the day of the official entry of the Allied Forces. He spent Christmas 1917 there.

At last, in February, he got a Ford car and a driver, but only after having appealed to his official superior, Charles Masterman, at the Ministry of Information in London. He drove down to the Dead Sea, and almost at once had to rescue Allenby, whom he found stranded, his staff car bogged in the mudbanks on the shore. April and May found him sketching in the Jordan Valley.

> What a sinister place that is. It is like being in a vast white oven, with, for a lid, the sky resting on the Moab Mountains on one side and the Jordanian hills the other. I'm going to have to rake through the Bible tomorrow, as I'm inclined to think the Hebrew idea of Hell, on which we were brought up, took shape from their living on the edge of this furnace . . .

> Watercolour is getting impossible, and I'm a bit tired of the medium. We are comparatively free from dust, but the appalling heat dries the blod immediately it is put on the paper, and buckles it, and a wash is altogether out of the question, so I have written to Masterman for permission to paint in oils also. I hope he will grant it.*

Permission granted, he set to work on a portrait of Allenby. By then he had sent back to the War Office 202 drawings, some of which were exhibited in London. But this was not all: the last few months of the campaign proved an exciting and prolific period. Thanks to the car, he kept well up to the front, as it moved from Nazareth and Haifa, through Tiberias to Damascus and finally Aleppo. Troops attacking, counter bombardment, 'pushed on to dressing station where saw many dead Scots,' Australian cavalry, a bombardment at Mulebis—'the dawn came in and with it the sky was sprinkled with shrapnel'—a Handley Page taking off, the burial of the dead, an aerodrome, Indian troops struggling for water, the first rains on the plains of Esdraelon—all this he saw and recorded, finally completing another 100 drawings. Some of these he later made into etchings: the dramatic images of *The Dead Sea*, flat and ghostly as a patrol approaches it by moonlight; and two studies of night bombardments, *Zero*, with silhouettes of a gun and three soldiers violently contrasting with the flash of a bursting shell, and *Gunfire, Mount of Olives*, in which the

* Letter to William Hutcheon, early 1918.

statue of the Virgin and Child on a hospital roof is caught against another blinding explosion. Several times McBey was reminded of Morocco. He saw a likeness to the North African landscape in the sandhills outside Askelon when he sketched a ruined village, and at dawn on the plains beyond Gaza where 'everything reminds me of Tetuan'.

Before he sailed for England, on 4 February 1919, he completed two portraits which became famous. Summoned to paint the new King Feisal,

> I was piloted to the end of a crowded room where Feisal was holding audience. He greeted me smilingly, and spoke to the interpreter, who translated: 'His Highness wishes to know where you wish him to sit to be photographed.' Tell him he is going to be painted, not photographed, and that he will have to sit steady for an hour, perhaps two. I half expected a refusal, but Feisal merely shrugged his shoulders, and uttered the Arabic 'Ma'alesh' (it does not matter). I lured him into a small room, away from the crowd. Feisal sat wonderfully steady for about five minutes, then he suggested lunch, and we adjourned. To my surprise, the many Arab Chieftains, lunching with Feisal, at an enormously long table, sat in European style, used knives and forks although the food was Arabic. A huge Abyssinian negro, with swords, knives, and automatic revolvers hung around him, stood immobile behind the Emir's chair.

After lunch the sitting began again and this time McBey placed him in a Savonarola chair in the corner. Feisal was evidently uncomfortable, for each time McBey looked up he saw the King trying to rise from his chair and he tried to indicate by scowls and signs, that he should not move. Not until the sitting was finished did Feisal rise, angrily throwing across the room a doorknob which had been carelessly left on the chair.

The portrait of T. E. Lawrence in Arab dress was painted in trying but moving circumstances. The sitting took place during his last days with the Arabs, and there was a constant procession of Sheiks kneeling before him and kissing his hands, many in tears.

McBey and Lawrence did not meet again until some years after the war, and then only briefly. McBey was at the Royal Academy and noticed a small figure which seemed to be familiar to him. Lawrence was standing before the portrait of himself, examining it intently. McBey thought that he was unrecognised but Lawrence turned to remark, rather sadly, that their last meeting had been in very different surroundings. He accepted an invitation to the studio that evening, but McBey had two friends to tea, and when they heard that Lawrence of Arabia was coming, they stayed on. There was no sign of Lawrence and at about eight o'clock they gave him up and all went to the cinema. On his return he heard that Lawrence had arrived about nine and had stayed talking a long time to the housekeeper. He told her that he had also come earlier, but hearing a buzz of conversation, had thought it was a party and decided to return later. The two men never met again.

McBey returned to success, recognition, and prosperity. He also acquired his first house, number 1 Holland Park Avenue, at the foot of Campden Hill. It had been bought in 1864 by John Galsworthy's father, a prosperous architect, for his daughter and her husband. Since the son-in-law was an artist, he decided to add a top floor studio. Doubtful whether the eighteenth-century structure could stand the extra weight, Galsworthy showed a Forsyte taste for solidarity and erected the studio on steel girders. McBey wanted the house very much, but it was a problem to find the money. He took his own collection of his etchings to Colnaghi's who in turn put up the money for him to buy the remaining fourteen years of the lease; a loan from George Davidson enabled him to purchase a further 999-year lease at a peppercorn rent. He cherished this house, the first he had ever owned. Immediately he devoted himself to restoring and improving it. He levelled the ground between it and the street, built a high wall and made a Dutch garden. He found for it antique floor boards and put in eighteenth-century pine panelling. Gradually over the years he collected piece by piece to furnish and embellish it, lavishing on it most of the money he earned and all his knowledge, imagination, and ingenuity.

His working hours were spent making etchings based on his war drawings of Egypt and Palestine. They were issued in three sets between 1919 and 1921, to great acclaim. For his drawings in the desert McBey had developed some of his most famous etchings, including *Strange Signals* and *Dawn: The Camel Patrol Setting Out*, in which he captured the dazzling light and some of the limitless space of the desert. Also in January 1921 *The Graphic* published a series of illustrated letters, written to William Hutcheon, in which McBey recorded his adventures in Morocco and as a war artist in the Near East.

The reopening of the Grosvenor Gallery in February of that year provided the occasion of his first exhibition of oil portraits. They were well received, and more commissions followed. One was from the staff of the North of Scotland Bank for a portrait of James Hutcheon, William's brother, which they wanted to give him on his retirement. It was he who had first shown an interest in McBey's etchings. He had been a remote and taciturn power in the bank, with a reputation for never speaking to his employees more than was strictly necessary. 'Why', McBey asked while he was painting him, 'did you never have a word for any of us at the bank, Mr Hutcheon?' The reply, still tight-lipped, was 'I did not want to show favouritism.'

He returned to Spain, to France, and to Holland, exploring the latter in a Dutch flat-bottomed sailing boat which he acquired to work on in peace. He quickly learned to navigate and maintain it himself. For the following six years, his life was to centre more and more around his boats—the *Esna* and then the *Mavic*, the Baltic ex-revenue cutter which he bought three years later. The continual entries in his diaries referring to sketching, painting, and the making of etchings go on, but now against a nautical background.

His work brought him new friends, among them Francis

Berry, a keen collector of etchings and a director of Berry Brothers and Co., the wine merchants. It was Berry's interest in art, not McBey's in wine, that drew the two together. One day in April 1923 Francis Berry told him over lunch that they intended to put on the American market a very fine Scotch whisky, and wanted a name and label for it. McBey supplied both, suggesting Cutty Sark and later designing the label for it. Francis Berry was delighted with it and it was at once adopted. Both name and label have been kept by the firm, and the term 'Scots Whisky' on which McBey insisted, instead of the more usual 'Scotch', is still used.

These were the days of the etching boom. Unlike other artists, McBey always did his own printing, controlling every stage of the process: 'When the artist himself prints, the printing may be regarded as actually a continuation of his etched work, the combination of both culminating in the finished proof.' By 1928 he had printed over 10,000 proofs with his own hands. He would not trust his plates beyond the eighty proofs, 50 for Britain, 20 for the U.S.A., and the rest for the artist, to which his editions were limited, but these were not nearly enough to meet demand. Saleroom prices mounted, as subscribers could not resist the chance of making a spectacular profit. Martin Hardie was to say later that the public had made over £250,000 on sales of McBey's etchings. The waiting list to purchase prints at the dealer's published price numbered hundreds, and the excess of demand was increased by the dealers, who would buy and hold back part of each edition as an investment. McBey received only a few pounds per print from his dealers, while his etchings were fetching hundreds of pounds in the auction rooms. Owing to the amount of publicity these enormous prices were given in the press, he was presumed to be a rich man. He did not, however, benefit directly from these speculative prices. *Dawn*, for example, for which he was paid £3. 10s. 0d. per print by Colnaghi's, once fetched £445, then the highest price ever paid for a print by a living artist at auction.

In September 1924, in his forty-second year, he went,

for the first time, to Venice. Countless artists have come to record the magical city and seascape, and it has enlarged their vision, stimulated them to reach for or perfect new techniques; it was to have the same effect on McBey. He came two years running and rented a flat overlooking the Grand Canal. Duncan Macdonald of Reid and Lefevre's gallery, a vivacious Scot and an enthusiast for McBey's work, came with him, and so, on the second occasion, did Martin Hardie.

> Every morning, during a month which I spent in his company in the autumn of 1925, he was out at five a.m. to see whether the sun was rising in mist or cloud, or in a sky of blue. He began at dawn; he spent hours at the end of the Rialto or at a table under the colonnade of the Chioggia Café in the Piazzetta, making pen and ink notes of figures; or in a gondola on the canals or the Giudecca, making studies of shipping, of buildings and their reflections; at night he would be out again in his gondola, working on a copper plate by the light of three tallow candles in an old tin! Never has anyone been less dependent on the orthodox paraphernalia of his craft. I have known a day's bag of an oil sketch, a brace of watercolours, several pen studies, and an etching.

Hardie also notes that in order to be able to draw direct on to plates without producing a reverse image, he would sit with his back to the view, studying it in a car mirror fixed to the side of his easel. He managed to work in terms of his own way of seeing and capturing impressions—no small accomplishment for any artist coming to Venice after Canaletto and Whistler. Light—the light of different times of day and night and different weathers, the complementary light in sky and water and on the walls of the city's palaces and churches—is a dominant element in these strongly designed etchings. On the last day he was loath to leave: 'Sketched from sandalo in canals but felt unsettled. No heart in it. Feel goodbye. Walked along to Dogana. Goodbye to Venice at night—clear moonlight. Goodbye while looking' (McBey had the superstition that, if he visually fixed a place or person in his memory on leave-taking, he would see them again).

The three sets of Venice etchings, with all their variety of techniques, some light and precise, others luminous and dramatic, were recognised as the summit of his achievement so far. The two Colnaghi partners, O. Gutekunst and Gustav Mayer, who had been vigorously pushing his work, were delighted with them. On 10 February 1928 McBey wrote in his diary, 'Mayer came up unexpectedly and bought trials of first eight Venice plates for £5,250.' Colnaghi's had not exhibited the series, preferring to hold them back and distribute them privately. It was Reid and Lefevre who gave the first show of them all in spring 1926. It was an immense success, both with buyers and the press. The *Morning Post* reviewed it with Colnaghi's simultaneous exhibition of Dürer woodcuts under the heading 'Dürer and McBey'.

It was Duncan Macdonald also who arranged for an exhibition of his oil portraits at Knoedler's in Chicago and persuaded McBey to visit America for the first time, in company with himself; they sailed on 16 October 1929. It was a bad time to come. The slump had started, and panic had just struck Wall Street. The exhibition was not a success, but he met the dealers who had supplied American collectors with his work, and through them the collectors. He found many commissions for etched portraits waiting for him, and much hospitality. At a reception given in his honour in Philadelphia, he met one of the three main collectors of his work, H. H. Kynett. He had already met Lessing Rosenwald and Albert Wiggin, Chairman of the Chase National Bank. All three were to become friends.*

He returned to England in March 1930 for a few months, then in October he sailed back to America. He had been encouraged by his collector friends to make a series of

* All three collections are now in public galleries: in the Aberdeen Art Gallery, National Gallery of Art, Washington, and Boston Public Library.

etchings of New York (not published till 1934) and worked
on them as before, in a friend's studio. He wandered up the
east coast to Boston and back, particularly captivated by the
little ports, to which he often returned. In November he
went to Philadelphia where he had commissions to paint
several portraits and the offer of a studio. Taken out to
dinner by the Sesslers, he met a dark and exotically beautiful
girl, Marguerite Loeb. They were immediately attracted to
each other. In January McBey joined Marguerite and her
recently widowed mother in Bermuda and two weeks later,
on the boat back to New York, he asked Marguerite to
marry him.

He was then just 47 years old—a powerful, energetic man
with an irrepressible sense of humour. His massive head with
its shock of greying hair, his strong and rugged features, his
vivid blue wide-set eyes gave him a most striking appearance. Although he spoke seldom about his art, it dominated
his life; he let nothing interfere with it. He was a strong man,
in character and physique—altogether, an alarming as well
as exciting prospect for a girl so much younger than he. Since
the affair in Cairo, McBey had been deeply involved twice,
each time with women who found him a challenge that they
finally decided not to accept. But Marguerite was in her own
way equally independent; each offered the other a challenge,
which together they found irresistible. They were married
quietly in New York on Friday the 13th of March 1931 and
sailed the same day for England.

Both being shy and disliking publicity, they kept the
marriage a complete secret. McBey had not told his friends
or even his housekeeper, and Marguerite's arrival created
awkward but amusing surprises (which McBey thoroughly
enjoyed) until the news leaked out to the press. The McBeys
were quickly known as 'a striking couple', a description that
haunted them for the twenty-eight years of their marriage.

That winter was a busy and happy one. They were both
working hard. Marguerite was an accomplished bookbinder
and her work had just been exhibited at the Golden Gate
International Exposition in San Francisco. She had shipped

her bookbinding equipment from New York and set up a bindery in the house. McBey realised that she was an artist in her own right, and encouraged her to paint, but, happy in her marriage, she was diffident of approaching the art of which he was master. After his death, she began to work seriously in watercolours and discovered the original talent which he had discerned. An exhibition of her work was held in London and Aberdeen in 1975.

In August 1932 they set off together for Spain. It was a journey which turned out to have important consequences. The sixty watercolours he made there were the subject of another successful exhibition at Colnaghi's the following year. Although this was McBey's third visit to Spain, now that he had a car and a tent he found a new freedom to sketch and explore the country. In Seville they settled in an old riverside house in Triana where McBey was able to work in oils, painting bull-fights and gipsies. Later they made their way south via Cadiz to Algeciras. From there, leaving the car, they crossed the Straits of Gibraltar.

Morocco immediately overwhelmed and delighted Marguerite as it had McBey almost twenty years earlier. They went first to Tetuan and then by bus to visit the Sunday market in the remote village of Alcazarquivir. Heat, dust, and flies made work impossible and they took the first bus north, stopping at Asilah, a little fishing village, once a Portuguese stronghold, on the Atlantic coast. Walking along the seawall they noticed a partly ruined building that overlooked a long terrace with battlements, from which eighteenth-century Portuguese cannon jutted seaward. They started immediately what were to prove fruitless negotiations to buy it and in consequence did not reach Tangier till night. Next morning, as they were to get the ferry back to Algeciras at 8, McBey woke Marguerite at 4.30. Walking through the still dark streets, they finally reached a broad plateau—the Marshan—and there saw the day break over the Straits, looking across to Spain. They determined to come back.

Next spring they returned and bought a secluded and overgrown garden on the hillside two miles west of Tangier.

In it stood a small delapidated house, the remains of a summer pavilion built by the Shareef of Wazan towards the end of the last century for his English bride, the remarkable Emily Keene. McBey restored the house and added a studio, finding a new and engrossing interest in building with the Moroccan workmen. Wandering below among the groves of trees, the grassy slopes and outcrops of rock on a big headland descending steeply to the sea, McBey felt at peace as never before. He came to love this place which he called Chereefian Rocks.

They returned more and more often during the 1930s. McBey also painted portraits here, of the widowed Shereefa of Wazan and the Sultan's uncle, Moulay Larbi el Alaoui, the closest of their many Moroccan friends. Through him the McBeys found another house in Marrakesh, built around two courtyards in the *kasbah*. They wandered through the *souks*, a source of lasting fascination and many pictures. They made expeditions into the interior, south of Marrakesh to the High Atlas and the desert. On one occasion Lord Rowallan (whose entire family McBey painted) came too, and together they crossed the Tizi-n-Tichka pass to Ouarzazate; the pass was the subject of one of McBey's most spectacular paintings (1936).

Back in London life was full. In 1934 Aberdeen University awarded him an honorary LL.D. McBey was painting many portraits, among them E. V. Lucas and R. B. Cunninghame Graham. He continued to haunt sale rooms, out-of-the-way shops, and flea markets, buying anything from a gigantic pianola to unset precious stones which he had made up to his own designs. He delighted in old and beautiful frames, and bought them whenever he found them. He never stopped buying old paper, in ever increasing quantities, until his collection became the best and largest of its kind in the world. 'The skin of old paper becomes soft and velvety, due to the action of time on the surface size, while the strength of the actual paper itself is not impaired', he wrote. He gave the same attention to the other materials of his art, experimenting with special inks for his plates, and importing the best paints he could buy from Belgium. His canvas was the best unbleached linen, which he bought in large rolls, stretching and priming it himself. He also studied the methods of early painters, and spent hours experimenting in different media and making up his own varnishes.

He had now evolved a completely new style of oil painting—a rather startling break-away from the conventional traditions. His painting was flatter and more tempera-like, his colours clearer but no less subtle, and he showed that he could use a calligraphic line as effectively in a painting as in his drawings and etchings. This style was first publicly seen in the exhibition of his paintings held by Colnaghi's in April 1937.

There were landscapes, *Tichka Pass: High Atlas*, *Sirocco* (a dust storm in Marrakesh), and *Ythan Mouth* (Newburgh); portraits of Gina Malo the actress, his friend Arthur Allen as *Chess Player*, his favourite picture of Marguerite, *Portrait of a Hero* (Johnnie Innes, coxswain of the Newburgh lifeboat in his youth), and a group of pictures of Moroccan women amongst which was *Angera Peasant Girl*.

In the late summer of 1939, the McBeys went to America to visit Marguerite's family. They had planned to return to Morocco, but on the outbreak of the Second World War, the immigration authorities impounded Marguerite's passport and they had to remain in the U.S.A. for the duration. With only a visitor's visa, deprived of his main income from the sale of his etchings, McBey found himself at the age of 56 virtually starting again. 'We feel like refugees here', he wrote in his diary. He was obliged to accept whatever commissions were offered, and to travel interminably in carrying them out; leaving the country so as to be able to return on an immigrant's visa, he chose to go to Havana and back. He tried hard to get another appointment as War Artist, but he was rejected on account of his age, and finally realizing that he must earn a living in the U.S.A., he became, in August 1942, an American citizen.

That autumn McBey and Marguerite started on a long and adventurous journey by car to the West Coast where they remained until the spring. Throughout the whole journey McBey made drawings and watercolours and subsequently produced two of the finest of his later etchings: *California, San Luis Obispo* and *Ranchos de Taos*. In San Francisco and Los Angeles he was a great success, and an exhibition of his work at the Pasadena Art Institute was enthusiastically received.

On their return he and Marguerite settled in New York and in October acquired a small studio house in Macdougal Alley, off Washington Square. Commissions for board-room portraits provided an income but limited satisfaction. Between them he found time for more personal work, etch-ings of New York and Cuba, including *Havana Harbour*. In 1943 the Smithsonian Museum of Washington held a retro-spective exhibition of his work beginning with *Boys Fishing* (1902), including the drypoint series of Spanish bull-fights, the Great War etchings, and the Venetian series, and ending with his recent ones of New York and one of Havana. He also, from long habit, visited the sale rooms; among the things he bought was a Victorian sewing table, which to his amazement he recognised. 'It was part of my life till I was fourteen, it being the pièce de résistance in our miserable abode. I knew that table like I knew my own thumb. The missing bits of inlay were still missing. No voice from the dead could have affected me so much.' He also bought for a song a dockyard model of a French second-rate man-of-war of 1725. Six feet long, it fitted with difficulty into their little house. But rigging the ropes (which he span on a model of a contemporary rope machine made by himself), forging an anchor by hand, and generally refitting the ship were a welcome distraction from war news and the constriction of life in New York.* Restraint was painful for McBey, to whom freedom of movement was an essential part of life. He could not wait to get back to Morocco.

Finally the day came, and on 9 May 1946 they took the

---

* This model ship, rigged by McBey, is now in the Maritime Museum at Mystic, Connecticut.

plane (his first) to Tangier via Lisbon. 'I am so glad that it is granted me to be here again,' he wrote in his diary, 'God, I thank you.' Yet at first, after the long exile in America, it was difficult for him to find his bearings. He turned to writing the autobiography of his youth. In painting, apart from a few beautiful watercolours, it was a creatively thin period. He kept the studio in Macdougal Alley, and returned to it several times to paint portraits. Finally he bought El Foolk, the hillside house that he first saw in 1912. Planning and supervising the improvements himself, he discovered a focus for his restless energy and kept a written and visual record of every stage: 'Marguerite and I laid the tiles in the studio.' They moved into the house on New Year's Eve 1949.

During the last years of his life, McBey spent most of the year in Tangier, where he continued to improve the house and garden. He travelled and worked as vigorously as before. He continued to rise early, eager to make the most of the daylight hours. In 1951 he made a long ink drawing of the view from his bedroom window: Gibraltar, the Straits, and the amphitheatre sweep of the bay of Tangier to the east. For the rest of his life he used it as a chart on which to record the changing points at which the sun rose at different times of the year. He returned to Spain, and other haunts of his youth, this time with the feeling that he should say goodbye. The last journey, in spring 1959, took him back to Aberdeen and Newburgh. On the wall of his bedroom at Tangier hung a section of the large-scale Ordnance Survey map, showing the parish of Foveran. He died on 1 December 1959, after an illness of only two weeks—the first of his life. He caught a chill and following a childhood rule tried to throw it off with exercise, chopping wood. But pneumonia ensued, and he was soon very ill. During the last days of November, violent storms raged, and he was worried that he could not see the sun rise. On 30 November, told that it was morning, he said, puzzled, 'But I don't feel refreshed.' It was perhaps the first time that the coming of a new day had not brought refreshment. To the end, next morning, he continued at intervals to sketch in the air with his stub of pencil.

CANONGATE CLASSICS